Vanilla

THE WATKINS KITCHEN COLLECTION

Winona, Minnesota
Winnipeg, Manitoba

Vanilla

THE WATKINS KITCHEN COLLECTION

WRITING AND CREATIVE DESIGN
Jeff Severson

RECIPE DEVELOPMENT AND TESTING
Rita Bechly

DESIGN AND ILLUSTRATION
The Green Edge
Burgandy Nilles

ART DIRECTION
Terri Lieder, Watkins Incorporated
The Green Edge

FOOD PHOTOGRAPHY
Lennon, Bausman & Fitzgerald

FOOD STYLING
Karen Hazarian
Genie Zarling
(except as noted*)

PRODUCTION
Pre-press: Encore Color Group
Printing: Litho Specialties, Inc.

Front cover photograph: Lady Baltimore Cake

Back cover photograph: Cheese Blintzes

Photo on page 7 by Silker Anderson Photography

*Scrumptious Vanilla Cheesecake photograph (page 26)
Food stylist: Cindy Syme

CONTENTS

BASICS
Building blocks to help you create a variety of delicious dishes
8

CLASSICS
From down-home favorites to international show-stoppers
18

BRUNCH
Morning eye-openers that will transform your home into a bed-and-breakfast
32

COOKIES AND BARS
A rich assortment of finger treats and cookie-jar staples
44

SAVORIES
Soups, salads, entrées and side dishes you never thought
you could make with vanilla
58

PIES, TARTS AND CAKES
La pâtisserie is open with a fantastic selection of baked goods!
70

DESSERTS
Decadent delights to end your meal with "quality calories"
88

CANDY AND CONFECTIONERY
Sweet treats for holidays and any occasion
104

INDEX
112

INTRODUCTION

"Ah, you flavor everything; you are the vanilla of society."
– Sydney Smith (1771–1845)

When the English author and theologian made the above statement to his daughter, Lady Holland, he was paying her a supreme compliment. For unlike today, when "plain vanilla" has come to signify "bland" or "generic," vanilla was always considered the ultimate flavoring.

In fact, vanilla is still the world's most popular flavor, lending richness and depth to a myriad of desserts, gourmet coffees, Chinese tea, English pipe tobacco, and liqueurs from Ireland to Mexico. Its submissive, mellowing flavor makes it a perfect "supporting player" in many dishes (which has probably resulted in its being labeled as "generic"), while its intoxicating, seductive aroma has made its essence a star in the perfume world. All things considered, vanilla is still the quintessential flavor. With a history and mystique as rich as its aroma, vanilla is anything but generic...or plain.

A HISTORY OF VANILLA

Vanilla comes from the seed pods of a tropical orchid (*Vanilla planifolia*) native to Mexico. The local Totonac Indians learned to process the pods, or beans, through fermentation in order to bring out the natural flavor components, then incorporated them into their diet.

When the Aztecs conquered the Totonacs and other indigenous peoples, they were so enchanted by the flavor of vanilla that they forced their

Vanilla planifolia

subjects to grow the beans for them as tribute to the Emperor. Vanilla beans were used as an aphrodisiac, an herbal remedy, and as a medium of exchange. Most importantly, the beans were used as a flavoring for a blend of powdered cocoa beans, ground corn, and honey, which became the legendary "nectar of the gods," *xocoatl*.

The Spanish *conquistador*, Hernán Cortés, became the first European to taste this mixture when it was offered to him in the Aztec capital of Tenochtitlan by the Emperor Moctezuma (or Montezuma) II in 1519. Cortés repaid the favor by killing Moctezuma, conquering his people, and claiming the land, its gold and its silver for Spain. The royal drink became known as "chocolate," from its Aztec origin, and the secret flavoring, *tlilxochitl*, was renamed *vainilla*, which in Spanish means "small pod" or "small scabbard," in reference to the shape of the vanilla bean.

Vanilla became immensely popular in Spain, but only as it was used by the Aztecs—as a flavoring for chocolate. In 1602, Hugh Morgan, the apothecary to Queen Elizabeth I, suggested that vanilla be used as a flavoring by itself. Elizabeth was so enamored of the flavor that during the last year of her life, she would eat only foods prepared with vanilla.

The popularity of vanilla soon spread throughout Europe, but nowhere so much as in France. The French adored vanilla, and used more of it than any of their European neighbors. It was there, in fact, that Thomas Jefferson was first introduced to the exotic flavoring, and loved it so that upon returning to Philadelphia, he had some shipped to him from Paris because it was unavailable in the United States. How ironic that a flavoring native to the New World would have to cross the Atlantic twice to get to Mr. Jefferson!

Unfortunately, only people with the means of a Queen Elizabeth or a Thomas Jefferson could acquire this precious commodity, for vanilla was astronomically expensive. The Europeans were desperate for a more accessible source of vanilla, and smuggled plant cuttings out of Mexico for transplanting to England, France, and some of their tropical colonies. The plants thrived, especially in the tropics, but would not bear fruit. It was rumored that Moctezuma had placed a curse on the plants, and that they would never produce for the marauding Europeans.

Actually, it was not a curse that thwarted their efforts, but a very small bee. In 1836 a Belgian botanist named Charles Morren observed the plants in their native habitat and discovered that the flowers were pollinated by the *melipona* bee, indigenous only to Mexico. Without this insect intervention, vanilla was impossible.

In 1841, Edmund Albius, a former slave on the French island of Réunion, came up with a process of hand pollination which became known as the *mariage de vanille*. He pierced the membrane of the flower with a bamboo skewer, collected the male pollen, then transferred it to the sticky female stigma. (It was later discovered that the Totonacs had been aware of this all along, and had used the same method hundreds of years before.) Albius' island of Réunion became the home of the first vanilla-bearing plants outside of Mexico. Vanilla plantations were established there, as well as on the neighboring islands of Madagascar, Mauritius, and the Comoros, and in other tropical locations like Ceylon and the Seychelles; French Indonesia; and parts of mainland Africa.

HARVESTING AND CURING

Vanilla is the most labor-intensive agricultural product in the world, with the possible exception of saffron (which is the only flavoring more expensive than vanilla).

The vines are grown from cuttings planted alongside "tutor trees" on which to climb. The trees are pruned short in order to keep the plants within reach of workers. The plants will not bear flowers for three or four years. Once the plants flower, they are tended daily, using the hand-pollinating method perfected by Albius 150 years ago.

Shortly after pollination, the beans appear, and require eight to nine months to mature. Just as with the flowers, the beans don't mature all at once, so the plants require daily attention. In some vanilla-producing areas, the beans are harvested early to meet demand and because of theft. This results in an inferior bean. If left on the vine too long, a pod will split and can no longer be sold whole, but can be used for extracts.

In Madagascar and Tahiti, the beans are plunged into hot water to "kill" them before the curing process; in Mexico, the process is begun in an oven. The pods are then laid out in the sun to bake for hours, then placed in air-tight containers to "sweat" overnight. This process is repeated for a few weeks, until the beans turn dark brown.

In Java (Indonesia) and Uganda, the curing process is done much more quickly, with the beans being cured over a smoky fire. This results in an inferior bean that is used only in lower-grade extracts, as with split beans.

After the curing process is complete, the beans are sorted and graded according to quality, length, and moisture content. Moisture content is quite important, for if vanilla beans are too dry, they lack flavor. On the other hand, the same is true if they contain too much moisture. Good moisture levels are from 18–25%. The world's best vanilla beans are called **Bourbon**, or Madagascar-Bourbon, named for the *Ile de Bourbon*, former name of the island of Réunion. This designation applies to all vanilla beans from the island group which includes Réunion, Madagascar, Mauritius, and the Comoros. Of this variety, the very best come from Madagascar, have moisture levels between 20 and 25%, and are the world's most expensive. Each bean is branded with the grower's mark.

Mexico and Tahiti also produce some excellent vanilla beans, but they are not as consistent in quality as the Bourbon variety, and the crops are too small to have a great impact on the world market.

Indonesian and Ugandan beans, due to their fire-curing process, have unacceptable moisture levels of 15% or lower. The top quality beans will either be sold whole or made into the finest-quality extracts.

MAKING VANILLA EXTRACT

Vanilla extract is made by chopping the beans, then immersing them in a mixture of alcohol and water, which is continuously recirculated through the beans until the essential flavor components are dissolved into the liquid. This takes about 48 hours. The resulting "perk" is then filtered into a holding tank, where it is aged, like wine. Sugar or corn syrup is added to mellow the alcohol and to assist in aging. Once bottled, the aging process can continue for two to three years.

Pure vanilla extract, by law, must be made with at least 13.35 ounces of vanilla bean per gallon of liquid, and must contain at least 35% alcohol by volume. This is known as "one-fold" vanilla extract. Stronger concentrations are used by professional bakers and industries; a "two-fold," or double strength, extract contains 26.7 ounces of beans per gallon, and so forth. The United States Food and

Drug Administration also allows vanilla extract to contain one or more of the following ingredients: glycerin, propylene glycol, sugar, dextrose, and corn syrup. A product containing less than 35% alcohol must be called a **flavor**.

Imitation vanilla extract is any vanilla that contains other than natural vanilla flavors. In the best cases, it is a natural vanilla extract that has been fortified with artificial *vanillin* (the chief flavor component in vanilla) and other ingredients designed to imitate and/or strengthen the flavor. However, most contain no real vanilla at all. Because it is called "imitation," it need not contain 35% alcohol.

Mexican vanilla, though cited as a favorite by the late chef *extraordinaire* James Beard, must be purchased with caution, if at all. Although Mexican vanilla beans may be of very high quality, the vanilla extract produced there rarely is.

A recent study showed that as many as 42% of bottled vanilla samples from Mexico contained a substance called *coumarin*. This substance, which comes from the tonka bean, smells much like vanilla and can make even a cheap synthetic smell like the real thing. Unfortunately, coumarin is highly toxic in large doses; it can cause liver and kidney damage, and has been used in rat poisons, as it causes internal hemorrhaging. In fact, the amount of coumarin present in a single two-ounce bottle of Mexican vanilla could kill someone. Additionally, Mexican labeling laws do not require the declaration of ingredients such as coumarin, so you don't know what you're getting.

Consider that Mexico barely produces enough vanilla for its own use, and that real vanilla, no matter its origin, is expensive. Accordingly, it is highly unlikely that the bargain-priced bottles of vanilla found in Mexican souvenir shops are really a bargain.

THE WATKINS VANILLA STORY

One company that has become famous for its fine vanilla products is Watkins Incorporated, of Winona, Minnesota. Founded by J. R. Watkins in 1868, Watkins is the oldest direct-selling company in the world. "Direct-selling" means that the products are not sold in stores; they may only be purchased from a Watkins Representative.

According to the best available records, The J. R. Watkins Medical Company began manufacturing and selling vanilla extract in 1895 (it may actually have been in the 1880s, but earlier records are quite vague). J. R. Watkins' dedication to quality was legendary; it was he who, with his 11-fluid-ounce "Trial Mark" bottle, instituted North America's first money-back guarantee. His vanilla extract, superior in flavor to even the best store brands, quickly became a staple of the farmhouse kitchen. Watkins Vanilla gained international acclaim when it was awarded the Grand Prix with Gold Medal at the Paris International Exposition in 1928.

Watkins has produced a variety of vanilla products over the past century, the most famous of which is **Double Strength Imitation Vanilla Extract.** Unlike other "imitation" vanilla extracts, Watkins Vanilla starts with the very best whole vanilla beans (no "splits"), all from Madagascar, and with moisture levels in the optimum range of 21–23%.

A vanilla "perk" is made, just as with a regular vanilla extract. Once "brewed," it is fortified with vanillin and other ingredients to make the flavor resistant to degradation by heat or freezing (both possible with vanilla extracts), and to make the product double-strength. The vanilla is carefully aged, and has a very low alcohol level (8¼%), which makes it even more heat-resistant.

The result is a product that is not only more economical than pure vanilla extracts, but whose flavor is actually preferred by most people (its flavor profile is a bit sweeter and more intense than pure vanilla). Needless to say, it is far superior to any other "imitation" vanilla.

For those who are willing to pay the premium for top quality, Watkins also makes a **Pure Vanilla Extract.** The same top-grade Bourbon vanilla beans are used in making a classic vanilla extract that easily stands up to the world's best. In a blind taste test, it was found to be far superior to the industry's best-selling pure vanilla (the panelists were divided between Watkins Pure and Watkins Double Strength Imitation as the overwhelming favorites). This fine product is recommended where true vanilla flavor, with all its delicate notes of tobacco, fruit and wood, is a must. However, it is not at its best in instances where extremely high cooking temperatures can damage the flavor, such as in commercial baking and candymaking.

Finally, Watkins makes a **Double Strength Imitation White Vanilla Flavor.** This crystal-clear formula is designed not to discolor white foods, such as frostings, whipped creams and wedding cakes. Because it is colorless, it contains no real vanilla (vanilla cannot be made clear); however, the expert blending of its flavors makes it a very close match to its darker sister, and its flavor stability has made it a resounding favorite with bakers.

Most recipes in this book do not specify a particular Watkins Vanilla, but some do. Those that do were designed to highlight a certain property of the vanilla indicated. Those that simply say "Watkins Vanilla Extract" were tested with Watkins' most popular product, Double Strength Imitation Vanilla, but may be prepared with any Watkins Vanilla. Conversely, if a recipe calls for Pure Vanilla and all you have is Double Strength Imitation Vanilla, feel free to make the substitution (you may wish to use a bit less).

Whichever Watkins Vanilla you choose to buy, you can rest assured that you have purchased the very finest...it's all Watkins has ever sold during a hundred years in the vanilla business.

B A S I C S

VANILLA WHIPPED CREAM
(Crème Chantilly)

You'll love the way vanilla can turn a bland, innocuous topping into a culinary delight.

1 cup/250 ml heavy whipping cream
2 to 4 tbsp./30 to 60 ml powdered sugar (depending on
* sweetness desired)*
1 tsp./5 ml Watkins Pure Vanilla Extract

Chill the small bowl and beaters of an electric mixer (if in a hurry, place in freezer). Beat the cream in chilled bowl until it begins to thicken. Add the powdered sugar and vanilla and beat until stiff. Do not overbeat.

Makes 2 cups/500 ml, 1 tbsp./15 ml per serving.

Note from kitchen: If you don't want to make **real** whipped cream, you can make the store-bought variety better by adding 1 tsp./5 ml of Watkins Vanilla to 2 cups/500 ml frozen, thawed whipped topping or when making packaged whipped topping. It will help enhance the flavor.

NUTRITIONAL INFORMATION PER SERVING: Calories 30, Protein 0 g, Carbohydrates 2 g, Fat 3 g, Saturated Fat 2 g, Cholesterol 10 mg, Sodium 2 mg, Dietary Fiber 0 g.

VANILLA CREAM FILLING
(Crème Pâtissière Vanillée)

This is the pastry cream used in such classics as cream puffs, éclairs, and Napoleons. Our version, made without egg yolks, is much lower in fat.

½ cup/125 ml Watkins Vanilla Dessert Mix
¼ cup/60 ml white sugar
½ cup/125 ml water
1½ cups/375 ml milk
1 cup/250 ml Vanilla Whipped Cream (page 9)

In medium saucepan, combine dessert mix, sugar, and water; mix well. Stir in milk and cook over medium heat until mixture begins to boil and thicken. Remove from heat and place plastic wrap on pudding surface; cool to room temperature. When cool, fold in Vanilla Whipped Cream.

Makes 3½ cups/875 ml.

NUTRITIONAL INFORMATION PER 1/4 CUP: Calories 90, Protein 1 g, Carbohydrates 11 g, Fat 4 g, Saturated Fat 3 g, Cholesterol 16 mg, Sodium 104 mg, Dietary Fiber 0 g.

VANILLA

VANILLA BUTTER

½ cup/125 ml butter, softened
¼ cup/60 ml powdered sugar
1 tsp./5 ml Watkins Pure Vanilla Extract

Combine all ingredients and beat until smooth. Use as a spread for sweet breads or muffins.

Makes ½ cup/125 ml, 1 tsp./5 ml per serving.

NUTRITIONAL INFORMATION PER SERVING: Calories 40, Protein 0 g, Carbohydrates 1 g, Fat 4 g, Saturated Fat 2 g, Cholesterol 10 mg, Sodium 30 mg, Dietary Fiber 0 g.

CUSTARD SAUCE
(Crème Anglaise)

The English call it "pouring custard"; in Italy, it's called *Zuppa Inglesa*, whatever you call it, this classic is delicious served over cakes or fresh fruit. You'll find two versions of it in this book: one on page 94, and a richer version on page 96.

CREAM CHEESE CHANTILLY

This is a *Crème Chantilly* with cream cheese, which adds a slight tartness like a *crème fraîche*. Use as a dessert topping over fresh fruit or cake slices. A similar one-cup recipe appears on page 74.

2 packages (3 oz./85 g each) cream cheese, softened
6 tbsp./90 ml white sugar
2 tsp./10 ml Watkins Pure Vanilla Extract
1½ cups/375 ml heavy whipping cream

Combine cream cheese, sugar, and vanilla in medium mixing bowl. Beat until smooth. Slowly add the whipping cream and beat until light and fluffy. Can be stored in refrigerator for up to 3 days.

Makes 2 cups/500 ml, 1 tbsp./15 ml per serving.

NUTRITIONAL INFORMATION PER SERVING: Calories 100, Protein 1 g, Carbohydrates 3 g, Fat 9 g, Saturated Fat 6 g, Cholesterol 31 mg, Sodium 50 mg, Dietary Fiber 0 g.

VANILLA GLAZE

1½ cups/375 ml powdered sugar
1 tbsp./15 ml butter, softened
½ tsp./2.5 ml Watkins White Vanilla Flavor
⅛ tsp./0.6 ml salt (optional)
2½ tbsp./40 ml half-and-half, more or less as desired

In small bowl, combine first 4 ingredients; add enough of the half-and-half to achieve desired consistency. Use for cakes, cookies, or quick breads.

Makes ¾ cup/180 ml, 1 tbsp./15 ml per serving.

NUTRITIONAL INFORMATION PER SERVING: Calories 60, Protein 0 g, Carbohydrates 13 g, Fat 1 g, Saturated Fat 1 g, Cholesterol 4 mg, Sodium 90 mg, Dietary Fiber 0 g.

VANILLA CRÊPES

～✐～

The classic thin French pancake. Cooked crêpes can be stacked between layers of waxed paper and frozen in a sealed plastic bag for up to 3 months.

2 tbsp./30 ml melted butter
1 ½ cups/375 ml milk
3 eggs
⅔ cup/160 ml all-purpose flour
1 tsp./5 ml Watkins Vanilla Extract
½ tsp./2.5 ml salt
⅛ tsp./0.6 ml Watkins Cinnamon

At least 2 hours before preparing crêpes, with a wire whisk beat together all of the above ingredients. Refrigerate 2 hours. Brush a 7-inch/18-cm crêpe pan (or any rounded non-stick skillet) lightly with additional melted butter; heat over medium heat until a drop of water sizzles and rolls off. Pour in scant ¼ cup/60 ml batter, tilting pan to coat bottom. Cook 1 minute or until top is set. Loosen edges of crêpe with rubber spatula, shaking pan gently to loosen. Invert onto waxed paper. Repeat with remaining batter; stacking crepes between waxed paper. Use to make blintzes (page 22), Crêpes Suzette, or other dishes.

Makes 12 crêpes, 1 crêpe per serving.

NUTRITIONAL INFORMATION PER SERVING: Calories 80, Protein 3 g, Carbohydrates 7 g, Fat 4 g, Saturated Fat 2 g, Cholesterol 63 mg, Sodium 140 mg, Dietary Fiber 0 g.

VANILLA

CREAM PUFF PASTRY
(Pâte à choux)

6 tbsp./90 ml butter
¾ cup/180 ml water
¾ cup/180 ml all-purpose flour
¼ tsp./1.2 ml salt
3 eggs
1½ tsp./7.5 ml Watkins Vanilla Extract

In medium saucepan, combine butter and water. Bring to a boil over medium heat. Stir in flour and salt; cook, stirring constantly, until mixture leaves sides of pan in a smooth ball. Remove from heat and allow to cool slightly. Add eggs, one at a time, beating vigorously after each addition until mixture is smooth and glossy. Stir in vanilla.

Makes 12 cream puffs or éclairs, 1 per serving.

For Cream Puffs: Preheat oven to 400°F./205°C. Using either a pastry bag or tablespoon, form the puffs on a greased cookie sheet. Using the back of a spoon, flatten any points. Bake for 25 to 30 minutes or until golden and crisp. Remove puffs from oven and cool on wire racks. Cut off tops and remove any moist dough. Fill with Vanilla Whipped Cream (page 9) or Vanilla Cream Filling (page 10). Replace tops and serve.

For Éclairs: Preheat oven to 400°F./205°C. Drop dough by heaping tablespoonfuls onto greased baking sheet. With knife or spatula, shape each into a finger 4 inches/10 cm long by 1 inch/2.5 cm wide. Bake for 30 to 35 minutes or until golden brown. Remove from oven and cut a slit in each to allow steam to escape; cool completely. Split éclairs in half lengthwise, removing any moist dough. Spoon or pipe in Vanilla Cream Filling (page 10). Drizzle with melted semi-sweet chocolate.

NUTRITIONAL INFORMATION PER SERVING: Calories 100, Protein 2 g, Carbohydrates 6 g, Fat 7 g, Saturated Fat 4 g, Cholesterol 69 mg, Sodium 110 mg, Dietary Fiber 0 g.

WHITE CAKE SUPREME

Don't buy cake mix in a box! This recipe is so much better, with the added satisfaction you get by making it yourself.

2¼ cups/560 ml sifted cake flour
1½ cups/375 ml white sugar
1 cup/250 ml milk
½ cup/125 ml vegetable shortening
3½ tsp./20 ml Watkins Baking Powder
2 tsp./10 ml Watkins Vanilla Extract or White Vanilla Flavor
1 tsp./5 ml salt
4 egg whites

Combine flour, sugar, milk, shortening, baking powder, vanilla, and salt in large mixing bowl. Beat at low speed for 30 seconds, scraping bowl occasionally. Beat at high speed 2 minutes, scraping bowl occasionally. Add egg whites and beat at high speed 2 minutes more. Pour batter into 2 greased and floured 9-inch/23-cm round cake pans. Bake at 350°F./180°C. for 25 to 30 minutes or until cakes test done. Cool in pans 10 minutes. Remove from pans and cool completely.

Makes two 9-inch/23-cm layer cakes or one 13-x 9-inch/33-x 23-cm cake, 12 servings.

NUTRITIONAL INFORMATION PER SERVING: Calories 270, Protein 4 g, Carbohydrates 40 g, Fat 9 g, Saturated Fat 3 g, Cholesterol 3 mg, Sodium 300 mg, Dietary Fiber 1 g.

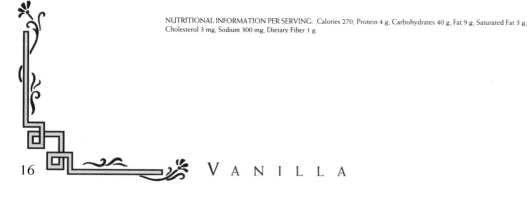

VANILLA

SEVEN MINUTE FROSTING

This light frosting is not only quick, it's fat-free! If calories are not a concern, and you want extra richness, see Cream Cheese Frosting (page 79) or White Fudge Frosting (page 81).

2 unbeaten egg whites
1 1/2 cups/375 ml white sugar
1/2 cup/125 ml water
1 tbsp./15 ml light corn syrup
Dash salt
2 1/2 tsp./12.5 ml Watkins Vanilla Extract or White Vanilla Flavor

In double boiler top, combine all ingredients except vanilla (don't place over water). Beat about 1 minute with hand-held electric mixer until blended. Place over, not touching, boiling water. Cook, beating constantly, until frosting forms soft peaks (this may take a little more than seven minutes). Remove from boiling water.   Add vanilla and beat until stiff peaks form.

Makes enough to frost tops and sides of two 8- or 9-inch/20- or 23-cm layer cakes, 12 servings.

NUTRITIONAL INFORMATION PER SERVING: Calories 110, Protein 1 g, Carbohydrates 26 g, Fat 0 g, Saturated Fat 0 g, Cholesterol 0 mg, Sodium 10 mg, Dietary Fiber 0 g.

BOSTON CREAM PIE

A timeless classic.

CAKE

2 cups/500 ml sifted all-purpose flour
1 1/2 cups/375 ml white sugar
2 tsp./10 ml Watkins Baking Powder
1 tsp./5 ml baking soda
1/2 tsp./2.5 ml salt
1 cup/250 ml buttermilk
1/3 cup/80 ml vegetable shortening
1/3 cup/80 ml butter, softened
3 eggs
2 tsp./10 ml Watkins Vanilla Extract
1 tsp./5 ml Watkins Butter Flavor

With an electric mixer, beat together all ingredients in large mixing bowl at low speed for 30 seconds, scraping bowl constantly. Beat at high speed for 3 minutes. Pour into 2 greased and floured 9-inch/23-cm round layer pans. Bake at 350°F./180°C. for 30 minutes or until cakes test done. Cool in pans 10 minutes, then remove pans and cool completely on wire rack. Place bottom layer on cake plate; spread with filling. Add top layer; drizzle warm glaze evenly over top of cake. Keep refrigerated.

Makes 12 servings.

FILLING

1/3 cup/80 ml white sugar
3 tbsp./45 ml Watkins Vanilla Dessert Mix
1 1/2 cups/375 ml milk
2 egg yolks, slightly beaten
1 tsp./5 ml Watkins Vanilla Extract

In medium saucepan, combine first 4 ingredients. Cook over medium heat until mixture begins to boil and thicken. Remove from heat and add vanilla. Cover with plastic wrap, cool to room temperature.

GLAZE

3/4 cup/180 ml white sugar
1/2 cup/125 ml Watkins Chocolate Dessert Mix
1 cup/250 ml boiling water
3 tbsp./45 ml butter
1 tsp./5 ml Watkins Vanilla Extract

In small saucepan, combine sugar and dessert mix; stir in water. Cook and stir over medium heat until thickened and smooth. Remove from heat and add the butter and vanilla. Beat by hand until desired consistency is achieved.

Makes 12 servings.

NUTRITIONAL INFORMATION PER SERVING: Calories 460, Protein 7 g, Carbohydrates 69 g, Fat 18 g, Saturated Fat 8 g, Cholesterol 118 mg, Sodium 460 mg, Dietary Fiber 1 g.

LADY BALTIMORE CAKE

Turn-of-the-century author Owen Wister immortalized Charleston's Lady Baltimore Tea Room in his romance novel "Lady Baltimore" after being served this glamorous cake by the Charleston Women's Exchange. Though the filling may vary slightly, this moist white cake is usually covered with a fluffy white frosting.

1 recipe White Cake Supreme (page 16)
1 recipe Seven Minute Frosting (page 17)
½ cup/125 ml chopped pecans
⅓ cup/80 ml raisins, chopped
⅓ cup/80 ml figs, chopped
¼ cup/60 ml chopped candied cherries, if desired

Prepare cake and frosting per recipes' directions. Combine ¾ cup/180 ml of the frosting with the chopped pecans, raisins, figs, and candied cherries. Spread between cake layers. Frost top and sides of cake with remaining frosting. If desired, decorate top of cake with additional candied cherries and chopped pecans.

Makes 12 servings.

NUTRITIONAL INFORMATION PER SERVING: Calories 370, Protein 5 g, Carbohydrates 60 g, Fat 13 g, Saturated Fat 3 g, Cholesterol 3 mg, Sodium 330 mg, Dietary Fiber 2 g.

VANILLA

SWEET POTATO SOUFFLÉ

A Southern favorite, used not only as a dessert, but also as a side dish for holidays.

3 cups/750 ml mashed sweet potatoes or yams
1/2 to 1 cup/125 ml to 250 ml white sugar
2 eggs, beaten
1/2 cup/125 ml milk
1 tsp./5 ml Watkins Vanilla Extract
1/2 tsp./2.5 ml salt

Mix together all of the above ingredients. Place in greased
6-cup/1.5-liter casserole; set aside.

TOPPING

1 cup/250 ml chopped pecans
1/2 to 1 cup/125 ml to 250 ml brown sugar
1/2 cup/125 ml all-purpose flour
1/4 cup/60 ml butter, softened
1 1/2 tsp./7.5 ml Watkins Nutmeg
1/2 tsp./2.5 ml Watkins Caramel Flavor

Mix together all of the topping ingredients; toss with a fork.
Sprinkle topping over sweet potatoes. Bake at 400°F./205°C.
for 30 minutes. Serve warm.

Makes 8 servings.

NUTRITIONAL INFORMATION PER SERVING: Calories 500, Protein 6 g, Carbohydrates 83 g, Fat 18 g, Saturated Fat 5 g,
Cholesterol 70 mg, Sodium 290 mg, Dietary Fiber 3 g.

CHEESE BLINTZES

2 packages (8 oz./226 g each) cream cheese, softened
1 cup/250 ml cottage cheese
1 egg
3 tbsp./45 ml powdered sugar
1 tsp./5 ml Watkins Vanilla Extract
1/2 tsp./2.5 ml Watkins Almond Extract
12 Vanilla Crêpes (see recipe page 14)

In mixing bowl, combine cream cheese and next 5 ingredients. With an electric mixer, mix at medium speed until smooth. Place 1/4 cup/60 ml cheese filling in center of browned side of each crêpe; fold left and right sides over filling and overlap ends to make a package; set aside.

TOPPING

1/2 can (21 oz./595 g size) blueberry pie filling (save remainder for another use)
1/2 cup/125 ml sour cream
2 tbsp./30 ml white sugar
1/2 tsp./2.5 ml Watkins White Vanilla Flavor

Heat pie filling over low heat; keep warm. In small bowl, combine sour cream, sugar, and vanilla; mix well.

To serve blintzes: Melt 1 tbsp./15 ml butter in 10-inch/25-cm skillet over medium heat. Cook half of the filled blintzes at a time until golden. Serve hot with warm blueberry pie filling and sour cream topping.

Makes 12 servings.

NUTRITIONAL INFORMATION PER SERVING: Calories 290, Protein 9 g, Carbohydrates 19 g, Fat 21 g, Saturated Fat 12 g, Cholesterol 128 mg, Sodium 250 mg, Dietary Fiber 0 g.

V A N I L L A

PAVLOVA WITH RASPBERRY CREAM

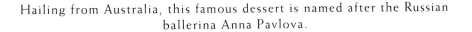

Hailing from Australia, this famous dessert is named after the Russian
ballerina Anna Pavlova.

4 egg whites, room temperature
Dash salt
Dash cream of tartar
1 tsp./5 ml cornstarch
1 tsp./5 ml Watkins White Vanilla Flavor
1 cup/250 ml white sugar

---

2 cups/500 ml Vanilla Whipped Cream (page 9)
2 1/2 tsp./12.5 ml Watkins Raspberry Extract
3 kiwi fruit
1 cup/250 ml fresh whole raspberries

In a large bowl, beat egg whites until foamy. Add salt, cream
of tartar, cornstarch, and vanilla. Continue beating until soft
peaks form. Add sugar, one tablespoon at a time, beating well
after each addition. Draw 8 circles, 3 1/2 inches/9 cm in
diameter, on a piece of parchment paper. Place paper on
baking sheet. Divide egg white mixture evenly between the
eight circles. Using back of spoon, shape into shells, forming
a hollow in center. Bake meringues at 250°F./120°C. for 1
hour. Open oven door, turn off heat and let shells sit in oven
for another hour or until completely dry. Remove from oven
and let meringues cool. Loosen from parchment paper and
place on individual serving plates. Combine whipped cream
and raspberry extract and divide evenly between shells.
Garnish with kiwi fruit and whole raspberries.

Makes 8 servings.

NUTRITIONAL INFORMATION PER SERVING: Calories 260, Protein 35 g, Carbohydrates 37 g, Fat 11 g, Saturated Fat 7 g,
Cholesterol 41 mg, Sodium 40 mg, Dietary Fiber 2 g.

HEART SHAPED NAPOLEON

This luscious dessert, found in the *pâtisserie* of Paris, was supposedly
the Emperor's favorite.

1 package (17¼ oz./489 g- 2 sheets) frozen
 puff pastry, thawed to room temperature
½ cup/125 ml Watkins Vanilla Dessert Mix
½ cup/125 ml white sugar
2 cups/250 ml milk
2 cups/250 ml Vanilla Whipped Cream (page 9)
½ cup/125 ml semi-sweet chocolate chips
1 tsp./5 ml vegetable shortening
1 cup/250 ml powdered sugar
1 tsp./5 ml Watkins White Vanilla Flavor
¼ tsp./1.2 ml Watkins Almond Extract
Hot water

On lightly floured surface, roll one sheet of pastry into a 12-x12-inch/30-x30-cm rectangle. Trace a large heart onto pastry and cut out with sharp knife. Place on baking sheet. Repeat with other sheet. Prick pastry well with fork. Bake at 400°F./205°C. for 15 to 20 minutes or until pastry is puffed and golden brown. Remove pastry to wire rack to cool. Meanwhile, prepare filling by combining the dessert mix, sugar, and milk.

Cook over medium heat until mixture comes to a boil. Remove from heat and cover with plastic wrap; cool to room temperature. Beat pudding until smooth; fold in Vanilla Whipped Cream; set aside.

Split each pastry layer in half to make 4 layers in all. Melt chocolate chips and shortening over low heat; set aside. Combine powdered sugar, vanilla, almond extract, and enough hot water to make a smooth frosting. Pour over one pastry layer. Drizzle or pipe chocolate in an attractive design on top; set aside. Place one undecorated pastry layer on serving tray; spread with a third of filling. Repeat with second and third layers. Top with decorated pastry. Refrigerate 1 hour.

Makes 10 servings.

NUTRITIONAL INFORMATION PER SERVING: Calories 480, Protein 6 g, Carbohydrates 56 g, Fat 26 g, Saturated Fat 8 g, Cholesterol 35 mg, Sodium 380 mg, Dietary Fiber 0 g.

CINNAMON FLAN

This classic baked custard, known in France as *Crème caramel*, originated in Spain, where it remains a favorite and whence it was brought to Mexico, the birthplace of vanilla. We've added Spain's (and Mexico's) spice of choice, cinnamon, for a new twist.
To make a classic flan, simply omit the cinnamon.

½ cup/125 ml white sugar
1 tsp./5 ml Watkins Cinnamon
7 eggs
½ cup/125 ml white sugar
Pinch of salt
1 tbsp./15 ml Watkins Vanilla Extract
½ cup/125 ml cold milk (not low-fat)
4 cups/1 liter hot milk (not low-fat)

Preheat oven to 325°F./165°C. Sprinkle ½ cup/125 ml sugar evenly over bottom of a small, heavy skillet. Cook slowly over low heat, stirring occasionally with a wooden spoon, just until sugar melts to a golden syrup. Immediately pour syrup into bottom of 1½ quart/1.5 liter round casserole, turning to coat all of the bottom and as much of the sides as possible (caramel syrup will harden). Sprinkle with cinnamon and let cool. In large bowl, whisk together the eggs, sugar, salt, vanilla and cold milk. Stir in the hot milk and mix well. Pour the custard into the caramel-coated casserole. Place casserole in a larger baking pan and fill with 1-inch/25-cm hot water. Place in oven and bake for 70 to 80 minutes or until a knife inserted in center comes out clean. Remove casserole from hot water and place on wire rack to cool completely; then refrigerate to chill, at least 1 hour. Just before serving, turn out into a shallow bowl or cupped platter that is about 2 inches/50 cm higher than the flan. Slice and serve, spooning some of the caramel sauce over each serving.

Makes 8 servings.

NUTRITIONAL INFORMATION PER SERVING: Calories 250, Protein 10 g, Carbohydrates 32 g, Fat 9 g, Saturated Fat 4 g, Cholesterol 205 mg, Sodium 120 mg, Dietary Fiber 0 g.

SCRUMPTIOUS VANILLA CHEESECAKE WITH CARAMEL TOPPING

A decadent cheesecake worth every calorie. Also, try the caramel topping on ice cream (pages 90-92).

CRUST

1 ½ cups/375 ml graham cracker crumbs
6 tbsp./90 ml unsalted butter, melted
¼ cup/60 ml brown sugar
½ tsp./2.5 ml Watkins Cinnamon

Combine all ingredients; mix well. Press crumbs over bottom and up sides of a lightly buttered 9-inch/23-cm springform pan with 2¾-inch/7-cm sides. Refrigerate crust while preparing filling.

FILLING

4 packages (8 oz./227 g each) cream cheese, softened
1 ½ cups/375 ml white sugar
5 large eggs, room temperature
1 tbsp./15 ml Watkins Vanilla Extract
2 tsp./10 ml fresh lemon juice

Beat cream cheese with electric mixer until fluffy. Gradually add the sugar and beat until smooth, scraping down sides occasionally. Beat in eggs, one at a time. Mix in the vanilla and lemon juice. Pour filling into chilled crust. Bake at 350°F./180°C. for about 1 hour and 15 minutes or until cake rises about ½ inch/1 cm over rim and center moves only slightly when shaken. Cool in pan on wire rack. (Cake will fall as it cools, sinking slightly in center.) Cover and refrigerate until well chilled, at least 6 hours.

TOPPING

⅓ cup/80 ml light corn syrup
⅔ cup/160 ml brown sugar
2 tbsp./30 ml butter
1/8 tsp./0.6 ml salt
⅓ cup/80 ml heavy whipping cream or evaporated milk
1 tsp./5 ml Watkins Caramel Flavor
½ tsp./2.5 ml Watkins Vanilla Extract

Combine first 4 ingredients in a heavy saucepan. Cook over medium heat, stirring occasionally, until mixture comes to a boil and all of the sugar is dissolved. Remove from heat and cool slightly, just until mixture begins to thicken. Slowly whisk in cream until blended. Stir in caramel flavor and vanilla extract; mix well. Let cool completely.

GARNISHMENT

2 cups/500 ml Vanilla Whipped Cream (page 9)
2 packages (1.4 oz./40 g each) toffee candy bars broken into pieces

To assemble cheesecake: Using a sharp knife, cut around sides of springform pan to loosen cheesecake. Release pan sides. Pour ⅓ cup/80 ml of topping into center of cheesecake. (Refrigerate and save remaining sauce as a topping for ice cream.) Chill cheesecake until caramel topping is almost set, about 2 hours. Just prior to serving, garnish cheesecake edges with an attractive piping of Vanilla Whipped Cream. Arrange toffee pieces in whipped cream border. Cut cake into small wedges. Refrigerate any leftovers.

Makes 16 servings.

NUTRITIONAL INFORMATION PER SERVING: Calories 560, Protein 8 g, Carbohydrates 49 g, Fat 39 g, Saturated Fat 22 g, Cholesterol 171 mg, Sodium 320 mg, Dietary Fiber 0 g.

BAKED RICE CUSTARD

A wonderful traditional pudding made easy with Watkins Rice Pudding Dessert Mix.

¾ cup/180 ml Watkins Rice Pudding Dessert Mix
4 cups/1 liter milk, divided
3 eggs, beaten
1 cup/250 ml raisins
⅓ to ½ cup/80 to 125 ml white sugar
2½ tsp./12.5 ml Watkins Vanilla Extract
⅛ tsp./0.6 ml Watkins Nutmeg
Watkins Cinnamon

Combine dessert mix and 3 cups/750 ml milk in heavy
2-quart/2-liter saucepan; bring mixture to a boil, stirring
constantly. Combine remaining 1 cup/250 ml milk, eggs,
raisins, sugar, vanilla, and nutmeg; gradually stir mixture into
rice pudding mixture. Pour into a buttered 6 cup/1.5 liter
soufflé dish or casserole; sprinkle top lightly with cinnamon.
Place soufflé dish in a large shallow baking dish. Add water to
a depth of 1 inch/2.5 cm. Place dish on oven rack and bake,
uncovered, at 350°F./180°C. for about 75 minutes, or until a
knife inserted near center comes out clean. Remove soufflé
dish from hot water. Serve custard warm or cold. Refrigerate
any leftovers.

Makes 10 servings.

NUTRITIONAL INFORMATION PER SERVING: Calories 200, Protein 6 g, Carbohydrates 33 g, Fat 5 g, Saturated Fat 3 g,
Cholesterol 77 mg, Sodium 170 mg, Dietary Fiber 1 g.

EGG CUSTARD

A delicious "comfort food" easily made in the microwave.

1 1/4 cups/320 ml whole milk
2 tsp./10 ml Watkins Vanilla Extract
4 large eggs
1/3 cup/80 ml white sugar
1/8 tsp./0.6 ml salt
2 tbsp./30 ml light brown sugar
1/8 tsp./0.6 ml Watkins Cinnamon

Place milk and vanilla in a 4-cup/1-liter glass measure. Microwave (HIGH) 2 to 3 minutes or until hot but not boiling; set aside. In medium bowl, beat eggs, sugar, and salt until blended. Gradually whisk in hot milk in a slow steady stream, stirring constantly. Pour into six 6-ounce/180-ml custard cups. Place cups on a 10-inch/25-cm round microwave-safe plate. Place plate on inverted saucer in microwave.

Microwave (MEDIUM - 50% POWER) 6 to 10 minutes, rotating each cup and then the dish 1/2 turn once, until edges of custards are set but center is still jiggly. Check for doneness after 5 minutes, then check every 30 seconds and remove each custard cup from microwave when set. Let stand at least 5 minutes or until center is firm. Sprinkle with brown sugar and cinnamon combination, to taste.

Makes 6 servings.

Note from kitchen: If a less sweet dessert is desired, eliminate the brown sugar/cinnamon topping and instead sprinkle with Watkins Nutmeg.

NUTRITIONAL INFORMATION PER SERVING: Calories 144, Protein 6 g, Carbohydrates 18 g, Fat 5 g, Saturated Fat 2 g, Cholesterol 150 mg, Sodium 120 mg, Dietary Fiber 0 g.

SCANDINAVIAN RASPBERRY SOUP

You would think that people who live in such cold weather would want hot soups, but Scandinavians love cold fruit soup, or *frukt suppe*, as an appetizer or a dessert.

2 packages (12 oz./340 g each) frozen raspberries (no sugar added)
*   or 5 cups/1.25 liters fresh raspberries*
1 cup/250 ml white grape juice
½ cup/125 ml orange juice
⅓ cup/80 ml white sugar, more or less as desired
3 tbsp./45 ml Watkins Vanilla Dessert Mix
1½ tbsp./25 ml water
1 tbsp./15 ml Watkins Vanilla Extract
Orange slices or fresh raspberries, for garnish
1 cup/250 ml sour cream
2 tbsp./30 ml white sugar
1 tsp./5 ml Watkins Vanilla Extract
Fresh raspberries or orange slices, for garnish

In medium saucepan, bring first 4 ingredients to a boil. Let simmer 10 minutes. Strain through a fine mesh sieve or cheesecloth to remove seeds. Return juices to saucepan. Combine dessert mix and 1½ tbsp./25 ml water; stir into juices. Bring to a boil over medium heat stirring constantly until mixture is slightly thickened. Stir in 1 tbsp./15 ml vanilla; chill at least 4 hours or overnight. Combine sour cream, sugar, and remaining vanilla; mix well. To serve, ladle chilled soup into serving bowls. Top with sour cream mixture and fresh raspberries.

Makes 6 servings.

NUTRITIONAL INFORMATION PER SERVING: Calories 310, Protein 2 g, Carbohydrates 59 g, Fat 8 g, Saturated Fat 5 g, Cholesterol 17 mg, Sodium 94 mg, Dietary Fiber 6 g.

WHITE CHOCOLATE MOUSSE

Serve this rich dessert in pretty parfait glasses with dark and white chocolate curls for garnish.

1 cup/250 ml vanilla milk chips or 7 oz./198 g white chocolate
1/4 cup/60 ml hot water
2 tsp./10 ml Watkins Pure Vanilla Extract
2 cups/500 ml heavy whipping cream
1/2 cup/125 ml sifted powdered sugar

Melt the vanilla chips in top of double boiler or in microwave oven. Add the hot water and vanilla; mix well until smooth. Let cool completely. Beat the cream until mixture begins to thicken. Add the powdered sugar and continue beating until soft peaks form. Stir a large spoonful of the whipped cream into white chocolate mixture; then fold into remaining whipped cream. Spoon into individual custard cups or a 4-cup/1-liter mold. Chill well; serve cold.

Makes 8 servings.

NUTRITIONAL INFORMATION PER SERVING: Calories 390, Protein 3 g, Carbohydrates 26 g, Fat 30 g, Saturated Fat 20 g, Cholesterol 81 mg, Sodium 80 mg, Dietary Fiber 0 g.

BRUNCH

PFANNKUCHEN (GERMAN PANCAKE)

This beautiful puffy pancake starts to deflate once it is out of the oven.
Have the topping ready so you can serve immediately.

4 large eggs
½ cup/125 ml all-purpose flour
2 tbsp./30 ml white sugar
½ tsp./2.5 ml salt
1 cup/250 ml skim milk
2½ tsp./12.5 ml Watkins Vanilla Extract
1½ tbsp./25 ml butter

Heat oven to 425°F./220°C. Combine all pancake ingredients except butter. Beat with wire whisk or rotary beater until smooth. Place butter in 10-inch/25-cm oven-proof skillet; melt in oven just until butter begins to sizzle. Remove pan from oven; tilt to coat bottom with melted butter. Immediately pour batter into hot pan. Bake at 425°F./220°C. for 14 to 18 minutes or until puffed and golden brown.

Meanwhile prepare Apple Rhubarb Compote (recipe follows). Remove pancake from oven; immediately fill with Apple Rhubarb Compote. Cut into wedges and serve immediately.

Makes 4 servings.

APPLE RHUBARB COMPOTE

2 tsp./10 ml butter
2 cups/500 ml sliced, peeled and cored apples
½ cup/125 ml thinly sliced rhubarb
¼ cup/60 ml apple cider or juice
½ tsp./2.5 ml Watkins Apple Bake Seasoning

Sauté rhubarb and apples in butter just until softened. Add apple cider and apple bake seasoning and simmer until apples are tender but still hold shape. Serve warm.

NUTRITIONAL INFORMATION PER SERVING: Calories 280, Protein 10 g, Carbohydrates 33 g, Fat 12 g, Saturated Fat 6 g, Cholesterol 230 mg, Sodium 410 mg, Dietary Fiber 2 g.

PEACH COFFEECAKE

The aroma of peaches and vanilla will brighten any morning.

½ cup/125 ml butter, softened
¾ cup/180 ml white sugar
1 egg, room temperature
1½ cups/375 ml all-purpose flour
1½ tsp./7.5 ml Watkins Baking Powder
2 tsp./30 ml Watkins Vanilla Extract
½ tsp./2.5 ml Watkins Peach Flavor
½ cup/125 ml plain yogurt or sour cream
1 cup/250 ml chopped fresh, frozen, or canned
    peaches, well drained
¾ cup/180 ml chopped pecans
2 tbsp./30 ml white sugar
½ tsp./2.5 ml Watkins Nutmeg

In large bowl, beat butter until smooth. Add sugar and beat until mixture is light and fluffy. Add egg; beat well. In small bowl, combine flour and baking powder; set aside. Beat vanilla, peach flavor and yogurt into butter mixture; stir in flour mixture. Add peaches and pecans; stirring just enough to blend. Spoon batter into an 8-inch/20-cm square baking dish. Combine remaining sugar and nutmeg and sprinkle over coffeecake. Bake at 400°F./205°C. for 28 to 30 minutes or until lightly browned and cake tests done.

Makes 12 servings.

NUTRITIONAL INFORMATION PER SERVING: Calories 250, Protein 3 g, Carbohydrates 30 g, Fat 14 g, Saturated Fat 6 g, Cholesterol 40 mg, Sodium 120 mg, Dietary Fiber 1 g.

VANILLA MUFFINS

These muffins are moist and delicious and wonderfully flavored with vanilla.

1 cup/250 ml white sugar
1 egg, beaten
2 cups/500 ml all-purpose flour
2 tsp./10 ml Watkins Baking Powder
⅛ tsp./0.6 ml salt
1 cup/250 ml milk
¼ cup/60 ml butter, melted
2½ tsp./12.5 ml Watkins Vanilla Extract
1½ tsp./7.5 ml white sugar
⅛ tsp./0.6 ml Watkins Cinnamon

Combine sugar and egg; beat well at medium speed of an electric mixer. Combine flour, baking powder, and salt. Add to sugar mixture alternately with milk, beginning and ending with flour mixture, beating well after each addition. Stir in butter and vanilla. Spoon into greased muffin cups, filling two-thirds full. Combine sugar and cinnamon and sprinkle evenly over muffins. Bake at 375°F./190°C. for 15 to 20 minutes. Remove muffins from pans immediately. If desired, serve warm with Vanilla Butter (page 11).

Makes 1 dozen, 1 per serving.

NUTRITIONAL INFORMATION PER SERVING: Calories 200, Protein 3 g, Carbohydrates 34 g, Fat 5 g, Saturated Fat 3 g, Cholesterol 31 mg, Sodium 120 mg, Dietary Fiber 1 g.

RASPBERRY AND CREAM CHEESE COFFEECAKE

Raspberry preserves and almonds top this delicious coffeecake.

Vegetable cooking spray
2 1/2 cups/625 ml all-purpose flour
1/2 cup/125 ml white sugar
1/2 cup/125 ml butter
1/2 tsp./2.5 ml Watkins Baking Powder
1/2 tsp./2.5 ml baking soda
1/4 tsp./1.2 ml salt
1 cup/250 ml sour cream
1 1/2 tsp./7.5 ml Watkins Vanilla Extract
1 tsp./5 ml Watkins Almond Extract
2 egg whites

---

1 package (8 oz./227 g) cream cheese
1/4 cup/60 ml white sugar
2 egg whites
1/2 tsp./2.5 ml Watkins Vanilla Extract

1/2 cup/125 ml fruit-only raspberry preserves
1/4 cup/60 ml sliced almonds
1/2 tsp./2.5 ml Watkins Cinnamon

Spray bottom and sides of a 9- or 10-inch/23- or 25-cm springform pan with cooking spray. In large bowl, combine flour and 1/2 cup/125 ml sugar. Using a pastry blender or two forks, cut in butter until mixture resembles coarse crumbs. Reserve 1 cup/250 ml of these crumbs for topping. To remaining crumb mixture add baking powder and next 6 ingredients; mix well. Spread batter over bottom and 2 inches/5 cm up sides of greased and floured pan. Batter should be about 1/4-inch/0.6-cm thick on sides. In small bowl, combine cream cheese and next 3 ingredients; mix well. Pour into batter-lined pan. Carefully spoon raspberry preserves over the top. In small bowl, combine reserved crumb mixture, almonds, and cinnamon. Sprinkle evenly over preserves. Bake at 350°F./180°C. for 40 to 50 minutes or until crust is a golden brown. Cool 15 minutes. Remove sides of pan. Continue to cool, or serve warm. Refrigerate any leftovers.

Makes 12 servings.

NUTRITIONAL INFORMATION PER SERVING: Calories 370, Protein 6 g, Carbohydrates 44 g, Fat 20 g, Saturated Fat 12 g, Cholesterol 50 mg, Sodium 280 mg, Dietary Fiber 1 g.

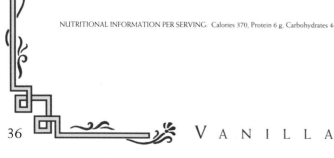

OVEN FRENCH TOAST

Can be prepared hours before serving and refrigerated until needed. This recipe can also be used for conventional skillet or griddle cooked French toast.

Butter
3 eggs, well beaten
¾ cup/180 ml milk
1 tbsp./15 ml white sugar
1½ tsp./7.5 ml Watkins White Vanilla Flavor
⅛ tsp./0.6 ml Watkins Nutmeg
8 slices, day-old French bread (regular bread can also be used)
2 tbsp./30 ml white sugar, optional
½ tsp./2.5 ml Watkins Cinnamon, optional
Pancake syrup, optional

Generously grease a 15-x10-x1-inch/38-x24-x2.5-cm pan with butter. Heat oven to 500°F./260°C. Combine the eggs and next 4 ingredients; beat well. Heat pan in oven 1 minute; remove from oven. Dip bread slices, one at a time, into egg mixture. Arrange on hot pan. Drizzle any remaining egg mixture over bread. Bake until bottoms are golden brown, 7 to 10 minutes. Turn bread, bake until golden brown, 3 to 5 minutes longer. If desired, sprinkle with sugar and cinnamon mixture; or serve with syrup.

Makes 4 servings.

Note from kitchen: To make ahead, dip and arrange bread in buttered, unheated pan; cover with plastic wrap and refrigerate 2 to 3 hours or overnight. Bake in the morning.

NUTRITIONAL INFORMATION PER SERVING: Calories 300, Protein 13 g, Carbohydrates 41 g, Fat 8 g, Saturated Fat 3 g, Cholesterol 170 mg, Sodium 470 mg, Dietary Fiber 1 g.

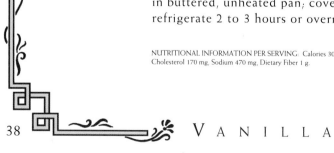

HOMEMADE GRANOLA

You'll want to keep a supply on hand not only for cereal, but also for snacking and topping yogurt and ice cream.

2 cups/500 ml old-fashioned rolled oats
½ cup/125 ml sunflower seed nuts
1 cup/250 ml flaked coconut
¼ cup/60 ml butter
¼ cup/60 ml brown sugar
¼ cup/60 ml honey
1½ tsp./7.5 ml Watkins Vanilla Extract
1 tsp./5 ml Watkins Cinnamon
¼ tsp./1.2 ml Watkins Nutmeg
½ cup/125 ml toasted wheat germ
1 cup/250 ml raisins
½ cup/125 ml dried fruit bits
   (apricots, raisins, apples)

On a large cookie sheet with sides, combine oatmeal, sunflower seed nuts, and coconut; mix well and spread out evenly. Bake at 300°F./150°C. for 20 minutes, stirring several times. While the oatmeal mixture is baking, in a small saucepan, add butter, brown sugar, honey, vanilla, cinnamon, and nutmeg.

Cook, stirring constantly, over medium heat until butter is melted and mixture is combined; remove from heat. Remove cookie sheet from oven. Increase oven temperature to 350°F./180°C. Add wheat germ to oatmeal mixture on cookie sheet. Pour warm honey mixture over oatmeal mixture. With a spoon or spatula, stir until mixture is thoroughly coated. Return to oven and bake 5 minutes more. Remove pan from oven and add raisins and dried fruit bits; mix well and spread out evenly. Return pan to oven and bake 5 to 10 minutes more or until golden brown. Remove pan from oven and pour mixture onto a large piece of foil; cool completely. Store in an air-tight container for up to 2 weeks.

Makes 6 cups/1.5 liters, ½ cup/125 ml per serving.

NUTRITIONAL INFORMATION PER SERVING: Calories 270, Protein 6 g, Carbohydrates 40 g, Fat 10 g, Saturated Fat 5 g, Cholesterol 10 mg, Sodium 54 mg, Dietary Fiber 4 g.

BREAKFAST SALAD

A simple dish for mornings when you want to treat yourself
or someone special.

1 unpeeled, chopped apple
½ cup/125 ml sunflower seed nuts
½ cup/125 ml raisins
¼ cup/60 ml chopped dates
1 sliced banana
2 tbsp./30 ml honey
1 tbsp./15 ml orange juice
1 tsp./5 ml Watkins Vanilla Extract
½ tsp./2.5 ml Watkins Cinnamon
1 cup/250 ml cottage cheese
4 melon halves

Combine first 9 ingredients; toss to blend. Spoon cottage
cheese into melon halves, top with fruit combination.

Makes 4 servings.

NUTRITIONAL INFORMATION PER SERVING: Calories 440, Protein 14 g, Carbohydrates 76 g, Fat 12 g,
Cholesterol 8 mg, Sodium 240 mg, Dietary Fiber 8 g.

CREAMY FRUIT DIP

Rich and creamy, this dip is a delightful way to dress up fruit.

1 package (8 oz./227 g) cream cheese, softened
1 container (8 oz./227 g) vanilla yogurt
1/2 cup/125 ml honey
1 tsp./5 ml Watkins Vanilla Extract
1/2 tsp./2.5 ml Watkins Cinnamon
1/2 tsp./2.5 ml Watkins Nutmeg

In medium bowl, beat cream cheese until smooth. Add remaining ingredients and mix until blended. Cover and refrigerate at least 1 hour to allow flavors to develop. Serve with fresh fruit dippers.

Makes 1 1/2 cups/375 ml, 2 tbsp./30 ml per serving.

NUTRITIONAL INFORMATION PER SERVING: Calories 130, Protein 2 g, Carbohydrates 15 g, Fat 7 g, Saturated Fat 4 g, Cholesterol 22 mg, Sodium 70 mg, Dietary Fiber 0 g.

CREAM CHEESE COFFEECAKE

This rich, delicious coffeecake is sure to be one of your favorite recipes.

1 cup/250 ml butter, softened
1 cup/250 ml white sugar
2 eggs
2 cups/500 ml all-purpose flour
2 tsp./10 ml Watkins Baking Powder
1/2 tsp./2.5 ml teaspoon salt
2 tsp./10 ml Watkins Vanilla Extract

FILLING

2 packages (8 oz./227 g each)
  cream cheese, softened
1/2 cup/125 ml white sugar
1 egg yolk
1 tsp./5 ml Watkins Vanilla Extract

TOPPING

1/2 cup/125 ml all-purpose flour
1/4 cup/60 ml white sugar
1/4 cup/60 ml butter, softened
1 tsp./5 ml Watkins Cinnamon

GLAZE

1/2 cup/125 ml powdered sugar
1 tbsp./15 ml milk
1/4 tsp./1.2 ml Watkins Vanilla Extract

Combine the 1 cup/250 ml butter and 1 cup/250 ml sugar; add eggs and beat well. In another bowl, mix together 2 cups/500 ml flour, baking powder, and salt. Gradually add to creamed mixture. Add vanilla; set batter aside. For filling, cream together cream cheese and next 3 ingredients; set aside. For topping, combine flour, sugar, butter, and cinnamon; mix with fork until crumbly. To assemble, spread half of the batter into greased 13-x9-inch/33-x23-cm baking dish. Spread with filling and spoon remaining batter on top; smooth with knife or spatula. Sprinkle with topping. Bake at 350°F./180°C. for 40 to 45 minutes or until cake tests done. When cool, drizzle top with a glaze made with the powdered sugar, milk, and vanilla. Refrigerate any leftovers.

Makes 15 servings.

NUTRITIONAL INFORMATION PER SERVING: Calories 440, Protein 6 g, Carbohydrates 44 g, Fat 27 g, Saturated Fat 17 g, Cholesterol 118 mg, Sodium 340 mg, Dietary Fiber 1 g.

BISCOTTI

This twice-baked Italian cookie is perfect for dipping in
dessert wine or coffee.

3 cups/750 ml all-purpose flour
2 tsp./10 ml Watkins Baking Powder
½ tsp./2.5 ml salt
4 eggs, slightly beaten
1 cup/250 ml white sugar
½ cup/125 ml butter, melted
2 tsp./10 ml Watkins Vanilla Extract
1½ tsp./7.5 ml Watkins Almond Extract
¾ cup/180 ml finely chopped blanched almonds

Combine first 3 ingredients, set aside. Beat together the eggs,
sugar, and melted butter; add extracts. Add flour mixture, one
third at a time; mixing thoroughly after each addition. Fold
in almonds. Spread half of the dough onto cookie sheet to
form a loaf 12 inches/30 cm long, 3 inches/8 cm wide, and
1½ inches/4 cm high. Repeat with remaining dough. Bake
at 350°F./180°C. for 20 minutes or just until starting to
brown around edges; cool 10 minutes. Remove loaves from
cookie sheet and place on cutting board. Cut across loaf
into ½ inch/1.3 cm thick slices. Lay cookies cut side down
on cookie sheet and return to oven for 12 minutes. Turn
cookies over and bake an additional 5 to 10 minutes or until
dry and crisp

Makes 48 cookies, 1 per serving.

NUTRITIONAL INFORMATION PER SERVING: Calories 80, Protein 2 g, Carbohydrates 11 g, Fat 3 g, Saturated Fat 1 g,
Cholesterol 22 mg, Sodium 58 mg, Dietary Fiber 0 g.

MEXICAN WEDDING CAKES

Nearly every Western country has a name for this cookie. Though Scandinavians will recognize *Smørkaker* as a Christmas staple, these buttery morsels are best known for their role in south-of-the border wedding receptions.

1 cup/250 ml butter, softened
½ cup/125 ml powdered sugar
2 tsp./10 ml Watkins Vanilla Extract
2 cups/500 ml sifted all-purpose flour
1 cup/250 ml finely chopped walnuts, almonds, or pecans
2 tbsp./30 ml half-and-half
Additional powdered sugar
Watkins Cinnamon

Beat butter, sugar, and vanilla until light and fluffy. Stir in flour, walnuts, and half-and-half, beat until smooth. Shape into 1-inch/2.5-cm balls and place on ungreased baking sheet. Bake at 350°F./180°C. for 15 to 20 minutes or until set but not brown. Cool slightly, roll in powdered sugar, set on wire rack to cool. To some additional powdered sugar, add cinnamon to taste. Roll balls again in cinnamon/sugar mixture. Store in well-sealed containers.

Makes 36 cookies, 1 per serving.

NUTRITIONAL INFORMATION PER SERVING: Calories 140, Protein 2 g, Carbohydrates 10 g, Fat 10 g, Saturated Fat 5 g, Cholesterol 20 mg, Sodium 60 mg, Dietary Fiber 1 g.

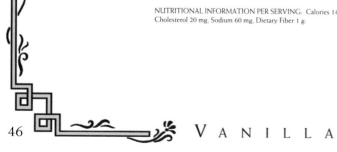

MACAROONS

A classic coconut macaroon flavored with a subtle hint of vanilla and orange.

4 egg whites
⅔ cup/160 ml white sugar
¼ cup/60 ml all-purpose flour
Dash salt
1 tbsp./15 ml Watkins Vanilla Extract
2 cups/500 ml shredded coconut
¼ tsp./1.2 ml dried orange peel

Preheat oven to 325°F./165°C. Grease and flour two large cookie sheets. In medium bowl, beat egg whites lightly. Add sugar, flour, salt, and vanilla. Stir in coconut and orange peel. Drop dough by tablespoonfuls 2 inches apart onto prepared cookie sheets. Place both cookies sheets in oven at same time, placing on top and lower racks. Bake for 13 to 17 minutes or until set and lightly browned, alternating cookie sheets after 6 minutes. Immediately remove cookies to wire rack to cool.

Makes 2 dozen, 1 per serving.

NUTRITIONAL INFORMATION PER SERVING: Calories 70, Protein 1 g, Carbohydrates 10 g, Fat 3 g, Saturated Fat 2 g, Cholesterol 0 mg, Sodium 30 mg, Dietary Fiber 1 g.

OLD-FASHIONED SOUR CREAM COOKIES

Your family will enjoy this time-tested classic.

3 cups/750 ml all-purpose flour
1 tsp./5 ml Watkins Baking Powder
½ tsp./2.5 ml baking soda
½ tsp./2.5 ml salt
1 cup/250 ml butter, softened
1½ cups/375 ml white sugar
2 eggs
1 cup/250 ml sour cream
2 tsp./10 ml Watkins White Vanilla Flavor

TOPPING
¼ cup/60 ml white sugar
½ tsp./2.5 ml Watkins Cinnamon

Sift flour with baking powder, baking soda, and salt; set aside. In large mixing bowl, beat butter, sugar and eggs, at medium speed of mixer, until light and fluffy. At low speed, beat in sour cream and vanilla until smooth. Gradually beat in flour mixture until well combined. Refrigerate at least 1 hour or until firm enough to roll into balls. Combine sugar and cinnamon; set aside. When dough is firm enough to handle, roll into 1-inch/2.5-cm balls and place on lightly greased cookie sheet. Sprinkle lightly with topping. Bake at 350°F./180°C. for 10 to 12 minutes or until lightly browned on bottoms. Remove cookies to wire rack to cool completely.

Makes 5 dozen, 1 per serving.

NUTRITIONAL INFORMATION PER SERVING: Calories 80, Protein 1 g, Carbohydrates 11 g, Fat 4 g, Saturated Fat 2 g, Cholesterol 17 mg, Sodium 60 mg, Dietary Fiber 0 g.

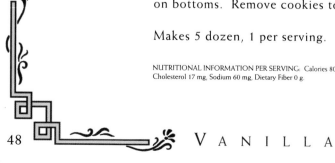

VANILLA

MOTHER'S OLD-FASHIONED OATMEAL COOKIES

These crisp-chewy oatmeal cookies will quickly become a cookie jar favorite.

1 cup/250 ml butter, softened
1 cup/250 ml light brown sugar
1 cup/250 ml white sugar
2 eggs, room temperature
2 tsp./10 ml Watkins Vanilla Extract
1 1/4 cups/320 ml all-purpose flour
1 tsp./5 ml salt
1 tsp./5 ml baking soda
1 tsp./5 ml Watkins Cinnamon
1/2 tsp./2.5 ml Watkins Ground Cloves
1/2 tsp./2.5 ml Watkins Allspice
3 cups/750 ml old-fashioned rolled oats
3/4 cup/180 ml chopped pecans
Powdered sugar, if desired

In large bowl, blend butter, sugars, eggs, and vanilla; beat until fluffy. Combine flour and next 5 ingredients; add to creamed mixture, mix well. Stir in oats and pecans. Drop by teaspoonfuls onto lightly greased baking sheet. Bake at 350°F./180°C. for 10 to 15 minutes. Cool slightly on cookie sheet; remove to wire rack to cool completely. If desired, sift powdered sugar over tops.

Makes 72 cookies, 1 per serving.

NUTRITIONAL INFORMATION PER SERVING: Calories 80, Protein 1 g, Carbohydrates 10 g, Fat 4 g, Saturated Fat 2 g, Cholesterol 13 mg, Sodium 70 mg, Dietary Fiber 1 g.

CREAM CHEESE SWIRLS

Swirls of cream cheese and chocolate team up in these delicious brownies.

4 squares (1 oz./28 g each) semi-sweet chocolate
5 tbsp./75 ml butter, softened and divided
1 package (3 oz./85 g) cream cheese, softened
1 cup/250 ml white sugar, divided
3 eggs, divided
1/2 cup plus 1 tbsp./140 ml flour, divided
1 tsp./5 ml Watkins Vanilla Extract
1/2 tsp./2.5 ml Watkins Baking Powder
1/4 tsp./1.2 ml salt
1 tsp./5 ml Watkins Vanilla Nut Extract
1/2 cup/125 ml chopped pecans, if desired

Melt chocolate and 3 tbsp./45 ml of the butter together; set aside to cool. In small bowl, beat 2 tbsp./30 ml butter and the cream cheese until smooth. Gradually add 1/4 cup/60 ml sugar, beating until light and fluffy. Add 1 egg, 1 tbsp./15 ml flour, and vanilla; mix well, then set aside. In medium bowl, with an electric mixer, beat 2 eggs until thick and lemon colored. Gradually add 3/4 cup/180 ml sugar, beating well. Combine 1/2 cup/125 ml flour, baking powder, and salt; stir into egg mixture. Stir in cooled chocolate mixture and vanilla nut extract. Pour half of batter into a greased 8-inch/20-cm square baking dish. Spread with cream cheese mixture; top with remaining batter. Cut through mixture with a knife to create a marbled effect. Bake at 350°F./180°C. for 35 to 40 minutes. Cool on wire rack; cut into squares. Store in refrigerator.

Makes 16 squares, 1 per serving.

NUTRITIONAL INFORMATION PER SERVING: Calories 190, Protein 3 g, Carbohydrates 21 g, Fat 12 g, Saturated Fat 5 g, Cholesterol 55 mg, Sodium 100 mg, Dietary Fiber 1 g.

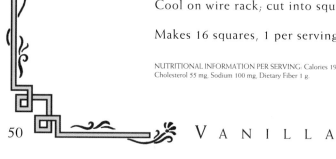

VANILLA

WHITE CHOCOLATE CHIP BROWNIES

The outstanding flavor combination of white chocolate, vanilla,
and macadamia nuts is perfectly complemented in these great tasting brownies.

BROWNIES

¹/₄ cup/60 ml butter
1 cup/250 ml vanilla milk chips
2 eggs
¹/₂ cup/125 ml white sugar
1 tsp./5 ml Watkins Vanilla Extract
¹/₂ tsp./2.5 ml Watkins Almond Extract
¹/₄ tsp./1.2 ml Watkins Nutmeg
¹/₄ tsp./1.2 ml Watkins Baking Powder
1 cup/250 ml all-purpose flour
¹/₂ cup/125 ml chopped macadamia nuts
  or toasted almonds
1 cup/250 ml semi-sweet mini chocolate chips

GLAZE

¹/₄ cup/60 ml semi-sweet chocolate chips
1 tsp./5 ml vegetable shortening

Grease an 11-x7-inch/28-x18-cm baking
dish; set aside. In small saucepan, melt
butter and vanilla milk chips over low heat;
set aside. In large mixing bowl, beat eggs,
sugar, and extracts for 2 minutes at high
speed of mixer. On low speed, add melted
vanilla milk chip mixture; blend well.

Add nutmeg, baking powder, and flour;
mix well. Stir in nuts and chocolate chips.
Spread into prepared pan. Bake at
350°F./180°C. for 25 to 30 minutes or until
top is light brown and center is set. Cool
completely on wire rack.

For glaze, melt together chocolate chips
and shortening; stir until smooth. Drizzle
over top of brownies. Let glaze set before
cutting into bars.

Makes 24 brownies, 1 per serving.

Note from kitchen: For a tropical twist,
add 1 tsp./5 ml Watkins Orange Extract
and 1 tsp./5 ml Watkins Coconut Flavor
when adding vanilla and almond extracts.

NUTRITIONAL INFORMATION PER SERVING: Calories 180, Protein 2 g, Carbohydrates 20 g, Fat 11 g, Saturated Fat 6 g, Cholesterol 23 mg, Sodium 50 mg, Dietary Fiber 1 g.

  V A N I L L A

NANAIMO BARS

These irresistible treats are very popular in Canada.

1 cup/250 ml butter, divided
2 1/4 cups/560 ml powdered sugar, divided
1/4 cup/60 ml unsweetened cocoa powder
1 tsp./5 ml Watkins Vanilla Extract
1 large egg
1 3/4 cups/440 ml graham cracker crumbs
1 cup/250 ml sweetened flaked coconut
1/2 cup/125 ml chopped pecans or walnuts
2 tbsp./30 ml milk
1 tbsp./15 ml Watkins Vanilla Extract
3 squares (1 oz./28 g) semi-sweet chocolate

In large saucepan, combine 6 tbsp./90 ml butter, 1/4 cup/60 ml powdered sugar, and cocoa. Stir over low heat until butter is melted. Remove from heat and add 1 tsp./5 ml vanilla and egg; mix well. Stir in crumbs, coconut, and pecans. Press mixture firmly onto bottom of an 8-inch/20-cm square baking dish. Bake at 350°F./180°C. for 20 minutes; remove pan to wire rack and let cool. Beat 1/2 cup/125 ml butter with remaining 2 cups/500 ml powdered sugar, milk, and 1 tbsp./15 ml vanilla until light and fluffy. Spread over crust. Over low heat on stovetop, or in microwave, melt together the remaining 2 tbsp./30 ml butter and chocolate squares; mix until smooth. Spread over filling. Cover and chill at least 1 hour.

Makes 24 squares, 1 per serving.

Note from kitchen: Try other Watkins Flavors and Extracts in place of the Vanilla. Vanilla Nut, Pineapple, Cherry, and Coconut are just a few suggestions. For a bar that is less sweet, melt just 2 tsp./10 ml of butter and 1 square of semi-sweet chocolate, drizzle in an attractive pattern over white layer.

NUTRITIONAL INFORMATION PER SERVING: Calories 200, Protein 2 g, Carbohydrates 21 g, Fat 13 g, Saturated Fat 7 g, Cholesterol 30 mg, Sodium 130 mg, Dietary Fiber 1 g.

TOFFEE SQUARES

These buttery bars have an easy-to-make chocolate topping.

1 cup/250 ml butter, softened
1 cup/250 ml brown sugar
1 tbsp./15 ml Watkins Vanilla Extract
2 cups/500 ml all-purpose flour
6 milk chocolate bars (1.55 oz./43.9 g each), unwrapped
1 cup/250 ml chopped, toasted almonds

In large mixing bowl, cream together the butter and brown sugar until light colored and fluffy. Add vanilla; gradually beat in flour until smooth and blended (dough will be stiff). Pat evenly into ungreased 15-x10-x ¾-inch/38-x25-x2-cm jelly roll pan. Bake at 350°F./180°C. for 25 to 30 minutes or until crust is golden. Remove from oven. Arrange chocolate bars evenly over top of crust; let stand 5 minutes to soften. Spread chocolate evenly over crust; sprinkle with chopped almonds. Cool, then cut into squares.

Makes 40 squares.

Note from kitchen: This recipe produces a crunchy bottom layer. If you prefer a softer version, add one egg along with the vanilla and reduce baking time to 18 to 20 minutes.

NUTRITIONAL INFORMATION PER SERVING: Calories 140, Protein 2 g, Carbohydrates 14 g, Fat 8 g, Saturated Fat 4 g, Cholesterol 14 mg, Sodium 50 mg, Dietary Fiber 1 g.

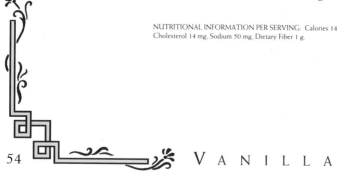

SOUR CREAM RAISIN BARS

These bars are very rich, so you'll want to cut into small pieces.

2 cups/500 ml raisins
Water
1 cup/250 ml butter, softened
1 cup/250 ml brown sugar
3 tsp./15 ml Watkins Vanilla Extract, divided
1 tsp./5 ml Watkins Cinnamon
1¾ cups/440 ml quick-cooking rolled oats
1 tsp./0.5 ml baking soda
1¾ cups/440 ml all-purpose flour
3 egg yolks
½ cup/125 ml white sugar
1½ cups/375 ml sour cream
3 tbsp./45 ml Watkins Vanilla Dessert Mix

Cook raisins in a small amount of water for 10 minutes; drain and cool. Cream together the butter, brown sugar, and 1 tsp./5 ml vanilla. Add cinnamon, oats, baking soda, and flour. Pat half of this mixture into 13-x9-inch/33-x23-cm baking dish. Bake at 350°F./180°C. for 7 minutes. Meanwhile, mix egg yolks, sugar, sour cream, and dessert mix in small saucepan. Bring to a boil, stirring constantly. Add raisins and remaining 2 tsp./10 ml vanilla. Spread raisin mixture over partially baked crust. Crumble the remaining oatmeal mixture over all. Bake for an additional 30 minutes. Cool, then cut into squares.

Makes 36 bars, 1 per serving.

NUTRITIONAL INFORMATION PER SERVING: Calories 170, Protein 2 g, Carbohydrates 24 g, Fat 8 g, Saturated Fat 5 g, Cholesterol 36 mg, Sodium 90 mg, Dietary Fiber 1 g.

DREAM BARS

~⌒~

Reminiscent of a candy shoppe favorite.

½ cup/125 ml butter
¼ cup/60 ml unsweetened cocoa powder
2 tsp./10 ml Watkins Vanilla Extract
2 cups/500 ml graham cracker crumbs
½ cup/125 ml powdered sugar
½ cup/125 ml flaked coconut
½ cup/125 ml chopped walnuts
2 tbsp./30 ml water
2 tsp./10 ml Watkins Cinnamon

½ cup/125 ml butter or margarine
½ cup/125 ml milk
½ cup/125 ml Watkins Vanilla Dessert Mix
3 cups/750 ml powdered sugar

1 bar (8 oz./227 g) milk chocolate,
  cut into pieces

In medium saucepan, over low heat, melt ½ cup/125 ml butter along with cocoa. Remove from heat and add vanilla; mix well. Stir in graham cracker crumbs, ½ cup/125 ml powdered sugar, coconut, walnuts, water, and cinnamon; mix well. Press mixture onto bottom of a greased 13-x-9-inch/33-x-23-cm pan; refrigerate.

In medium saucepan over low heat, melt remaining ½ cup/125 ml butter. Blend in milk and dessert mix. Cook, **stirring constantly**, until mixture thickens slightly, about 5 minutes. Remove from heat; beat in powdered sugar until smooth. Spread over crust; refrigerate 20 to 30 minutes or until set. In small saucepan, over low heat, melt chocolate, stirring constantly. Spread evenly over filling. Refrigerate 10 to 15 minutes to set chocolate. Cut into squares and store in refrigerator.

Makes 36 bars, 1 per serving.

NUTRITIONAL INFORMATION PER SERVING: Calories 170, Protein 1 g, Carbohydrates 22 g, Fat 9 g, Saturated Fat 5 g, Cholesterol 16 mg, Sodium 120 mg, Dietary Fiber 1 g.

VANILLA

$1,000,000 BARS

Butter, brown sugar, chocolate and vanilla combine to make this delicious bar ten times richer than the famous candy bar.

1 cup/250 ml butter, softened
2 cups/500 ml brown sugar
2 eggs
2 tsp./10 ml Watkins Vanilla Extract
1 tsp./5 ml Watkins Almond Extract
2½ cups/625 ml all-purpose flour
1 tsp./5 ml baking soda
1 tsp./5 ml salt
3 cups/750 ml quick-cooking rolled oats

FILLING

1 package (12 oz./340 g) chocolate chips
1 can (14 oz./397 g) sweetened condensed milk
2 tbsp./30 ml butter
½ tsp./0.5 ml salt
1 cup/250 ml chopped walnuts
2 tsp./10 ml Watkins Vanilla Nut Extract

In large bowl, cream the butter and brown sugar until light and fluffy. Beat in the eggs and vanilla and almond extracts. Sift together the flour, baking soda, and salt; stir in oatmeal. Add dry ingredients to the creamed mixture and set aside.

To make the chocolate filling, in medium saucepan mix the chocolate chips, sweetened condensed milk, butter, and salt and melt over low heat. Add the walnuts and vanilla nut extract. Spread half of the oatmeal mixture in the bottom of a greased 13-x9-inch/33-x23-cm baking dish. Cover with chocolate mixture; dot with the remaining oatmeal mixture. Bake at 350°F./180°C. for 25 to 30 minutes or until golden brown.

Makes 48 bars, 1 per serving.

NUTRITIONAL INFORMATION PER SERVING: Calories 200, Protein 3 g, Carbohydrates 26 g, Fat 10 g, Saturated Fat 5 g, Cholesterol 23 mg, Sodium 140 mg, Dietary Fiber 1 g.

CREAM OF CHICKEN AND VANILLA SOUP

An unusual but very delicious combination.

2 tsp./10 ml Watkins Onion Liquid Spice
½ cup/125 ml finely chopped celery
½ cup/125 ml finely chopped green onion
½ cup/125 ml all-purpose flour
1 cup/250 ml Watkins Cream Soup Base
2 cups/500 ml milk
3 cups/750 ml water
1½ tbsp./25 ml Watkins Pure Vanilla Extract
2 cups/500 ml finely sliced cooked white chicken meat
Salt and Watkins Black Pepper, to taste

In medium saucepan, sauté the celery and onion in Onion Liquid Spice until crisp-tender. Add flour, soup base, milk and water; mix well. Continue to cook over medium heat until mixture beings to boil and thicken. Add vanilla, chicken, and salt and pepper to taste; heat through.

Makes 8 servings.

NUTRITIONAL INFORMATION PER SERVING: Calories 170, Protein 7 g, Carbohydrates 13 g, Fat 12 g, Saturated Fat 1 g, Cholesterol 29 mg, Sodium 970 mg, Dietary Fiber 0 g.

CREAM OF CARROT SOUP

Vanilla enhances the natural sweetness of sautéed carrots and onions in this unique soup.

2 tbsp./30 ml butter
4 cups/1 liter chopped carrot (about 1 pound/454 g)
1 cup/250 ml chopped onion
½ cup/125 ml uncooked long grain white rice
1 tbsp./15 ml Watkins Vanilla Extract
4½ cups/1.15 liters water, divided
⅓ cup/80 ml Watkins Chicken Soup Base
1 cup/250 ml milk
1 tbsp./15 ml butter
Salt and Watkins Black Pepper, to taste
Watkins Nutmeg, for garnish

Melt butter in large saucepan. Sauté carrot and onion for 5 minutes. Stir in the rice, vanilla, 4 cups/1 liter water, and soup base. Bring mixture to a boil, stirring occasionally. Reduce heat and simmer for 30 to 40 minutes or until carrots are tender. Place half of this mixture in food processor or blender along with the ½ cup/125 ml water; process until smooth. Return to saucepan along with milk, butter, salt and pepper. Heat through, but do not boil. Serve hot with a sprinkling of nutmeg on top.

Makes 8 servings.

Note from kitchen: If desired, all of the soup can be put through food processor or blender.

NUTRITIONAL INFORMATION PER SERVING: Calories 150, Protein 4 g, Carbohydrates 20 g, Fat 6 g, Saturated Fat 3 g, Cholesterol 16 mg, Sodium 630 mg, Dietary Fiber 2 g.

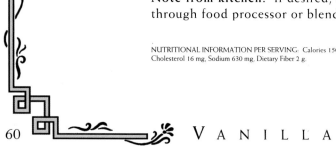

V A N I L L A

HAM WITH APRICOTS IN VANILLA SAUCE

Dried apricots give a sweet-tart taste to this vanilla-glazed ham.

*2 center-cut ham slices about ½-inch/1.3-cm thick (trim fat
and slash edge)*
1½ cups/375 ml dried apricots
1⅓ cups/330 ml water
3 tbsp./45 ml white sugar
1 tbsp./15 ml Watkins Vanilla Extract
¼ tsp./1.2 ml Watkins Nutmeg
⅛ tsp./0.6 ml Watkins Cloves
2 tbsp./30 ml Vanilla Dessert Mix
2 tbsp./30 ml water

Place ham slices in large glass baking dish. Bake, uncovered,
at 350°F./180°C. for 15 minutes. While ham is baking,
combine apricots and next 5 ingredients in medium saucepan.
Bring mixture to a boil; reduce heat and simmer 5 minutes.
Combine dessert mix and water; stir into apricot mixture and
cook until mixture begins to thicken. Drain excess liquid from
ham. Spoon apricot mixture evenly over ham slices. Bake an
additional 10 to 15 minutes or until heated through. With
two spatulas, remove ham slices along with apricot topping
to serving platter.

Makes 8 servings.

NUTRITIONAL INFORMATION PER SERVING: Calories 270, Protein 29 g, Carbohydrates 22 g, Fat 6 g, Saturated Fat 2 g,
Cholesterol 62 mg, Sodium 1,540 mg, Dietary Fiber 2 g.

TOSSED SALAD WITH RASPBERRY-VANILLA VINAIGRETTE

An elegant, fruity dressing gives this colorful salad a unique flavor sensation.

VINAIGRETTE

⅓ cup/80 ml olive oil
¼ cup/60 ml white wine vinegar
2½ tbsp./37.5 ml white sugar
2 tsp./10 ml Watkins Pure Vanilla Extract
½ tsp./2.5 ml Watkins Raspberry Extract

Combine all ingredients; mix well and chill until serving time.

SALAD

8 cups/2 liters mixed fresh greens
   (red leaf lettuce, escarole, radicchio, etc.)
1 small red onion, thinly sliced
1 cucumber, thinly sliced
1 cup/250 ml alfalfa sprouts
Shredded carrot, if desired
Salt and Watkins Black Pepper, to taste

Wash greens and break into bite-size pieces. Place in a bowl and toss. Add onion and cucumber slices, alfalfa sprouts, and carrot. Toss with vinaigrette. Season with salt and pepper.

Makes 8 servings.

NUTRITIONAL INFORMATION PER SERVING: Calories 120, Protein 1 g, Carbohydrates 8 g, Fat 9 g, Saturated Fat 1 g, Cholesterol 0 mg, Sodium 6 mg, Dietary Fiber 2 g.

VANILLA CURRIED CHICKEN

Just a hint of vanilla comes through in this spicy dish. Though vanilla is not traditionally used in India, it blends well with cinnamon and adds a haunting mystique to the complexity of curry.

1 cup/250 ml chopped onion
1½ tbsp./25 ml Watkins Ginger Garlic Liquid Spice
3 tbsp./45 ml all-purpose flour
1 tbsp./15 ml Watkins Curry Powder, more if desired
1 tbsp./15 ml Watkins Chicken Soup Base
1½ tsp./7.5 ml brown sugar
¾ tsp./4 ml Watkins Cinnamon
⅛ tsp./0.6 ml Watkins Cayenne (Red) Pepper
2 cups/500 ml milk
1 tbsp./15 ml Watkins Pure Vanilla Extract
½ tsp./2.5 ml Watkins Coconut Flavor
4 cups/1 liter cubed cooked chicken
Sliced pineapple or limes, for garnish
Toasted sliced almonds or coconut, for garnish
4 cups/1 liter hot cooked rice
 (Try one of Watkins Harvest Treasures Rice Medleys)

In large skillet, sauté the onion in the liquid spice until softened. Add flour and next 5 ingredients; continue to cook, stirring constantly, for 1 minute. Remove from heat. Combine the milk, vanilla, and coconut flavor; slowly stir into curry mixture. Bring to a boil over medium heat; add chicken and cook just until heated through. To serve, place hot cooked rice on serving platter. Ladle Vanilla Curried Chicken on top. Garnish with pineapple and lime slices. Sprinkle with toasted almonds.

Makes 8 servings.

NUTRITIONAL INFORMATION PER SERVING: Calories 350, Protein 25 g, Carbohydrates 37 g, Fat 10 g, Saturated Fat 3 g, Cholesterol 66 mg, Sodium 190 mg, Dietary Fiber 1 g.

HONEY AND VANILLA GLAZED CARROTS

This glaze is also delicious on yams or sweet potatoes.

¼ cup/60 ml butter or margarine
¼ cup/60 ml honey
1½ tsp./7.5 ml Watkins Vanilla Extract
Pinch Watkins Ginger
Salt and Watkins Black Pepper, to taste
1½ pounds/680 g baby carrots (about 5 cups/1.25 liter)
    cooked until crisp-tender

Melt butter in medium saucepan. Add honey and stir until
blended. Add vanilla, ginger, and carrots. Cook slowly,
stirring occasionally, until carrots are well glazed. Season
with salt and pepper.

Makes 5 cups/1.25 liters, 10 servings.

NUTRITIONAL INFORMATION PER SERVING: Calories 100, Protein 1 g, Carbohydrates 14 g, Fat 5 g, Saturated Fat 3 g,
Cholesterol 12 mg, Sodium 60 mg, Dietary Fiber 2 g.

TAHITIAN CHICKEN

The island of Tahiti is becoming increasingly well-known for its vanilla production. You'll love the subtle tropical notes in this easy-to-make dish, reminiscent of the South Pacific.

8 chicken thighs, skin removed or skinless,
   boneless chicken breast halves
¼ cup/60 ml all-purpose flour
1 tsp./5 ml Watkins Paprika
1 tsp./5 ml Watkins Seasoning Salt
⅛ tsp./0.6 ml Watkins Black Pepper
¼ cup/60 ml butter
¾ cup/180 ml orange juice
¼ cup/60 ml orange marmalade
2 tbsp./30 ml Watkins Tropical Salsa
½ cup/125 ml water
3 tbsp./45 ml Watkins Vanilla Dessert Mix
1 tbsp./15 ml Watkins Vanilla Extract
¼ cup/60 ml sliced almonds, if desired
4 cups/1 liter hot cooked rice (Try one of
   Watkins Harvest Treasures Rice Medleys)

Rinse chicken; set aside. Combine flour and next 3 ingredients; mix well. Coat chicken thighs on both sides with flour mixture. In skillet, melt butter and brown both sides of chicken. Place chicken in 13-x9-inch/33-x23-cm baking dish. To same skillet, add orange juice, marmalade, and Tropical Salsa; heat until marmalade melts stirring up any browned bits. Combine water, dessert mix, and vanilla; stir into orange juice mixture. Cook, stirring constantly, until mixture begins to thicken.

Pour sauce over chicken. Sprinkle with almonds. Bake at 350°F./180°C. for 50 to 60 minutes or until chicken is done. Serve over hot cooked rice.

Makes 8 servings.

NUTRITIONAL INFORMATION PER SERVING: Calories 360, Protein 18 g, Carbohydrates 47 g, Fat 10 g, Saturated Fat 5 g, Cholesterol 73 mg, Sodium 350 mg, Dietary Fiber 1 g.

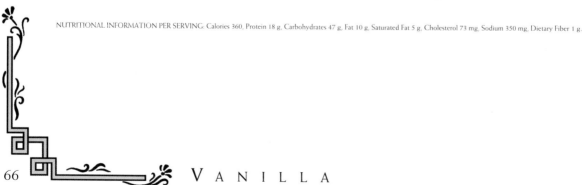

ALMOND AND VANILLA GREEN BEANS

Sliced almonds top these crisp-tender green beans flavored with a touch of vanilla. An enchanting side dish; the French would appreciate this treatment of their beloved *haricots verts*.

1 ½ pounds/680 g fresh green beans, trimmed
⅓ cup/80 ml sliced almonds
¼ cup/60 ml butter
2 ½ tsp./12.5 ml Watkins Vanilla Extract
Salt and Watkins Black Pepper, to taste

Cook beans until crisp-tender; drain well and keep warm. In small skillet, sauté the almonds in butter until golden brown. Remove from heat and add the vanilla, salt and pepper. Pour over beans; serve hot.

Makes 4 ½ cups/1.15 liters, 9 servings.

NUTRITIONAL INFORMATION PER SERVING: Calories 90, Protein 2 g, Carbohydrates 6 g, Fat 7 g, Saturated Fat 3 g, Cholesterol 14 mg, Sodium 50 mg, Dietary Fiber 2 g.

SEAFOOD SALAD
WITH VANILLA MAYONNAISE

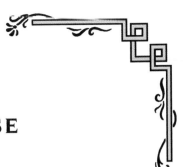

A very colorful and delicious salad, in which the natural acidity of mayonnaise and mustard is softened and rounded with a kiss of vanilla.

¾ pound/340 g medium-sized cooked and peeled shrimp
¾ pound/340 g imitation crab, broken into bite-size pieces
1 cup/250 ml cherry tomatoes, halved and seeded
1 cup/250 ml sliced fresh mushrooms
½ cup/125 ml sliced green onion
½ cup/125 ml sliced celery
½ cup/125 ml pecan halves
½ cup/125 ml mayonnaise
1 tsp./5 ml Watkins Parisienne Mustard
2 tsp./10 ml Watkins Vanilla Extract
Leaf lettuce

In large bowl, combine first 7 ingredients. In small bowl, combine mayonnaise, mustard, and vanilla; mix well. Toss into shrimp mixture; refrigerate until serving time. To serve, place lettuce on serving plate(s) and top with Seafood Salad.

Makes 8 servings.

NUTRITIONAL INFORMATION PER SERVING: Calories 250, Protein 15 g, Carbohydrates 9 g, Fat 16 g, Saturated Fat 2 g, Cholesterol 99 mg, Sodium 620 mg, Dietary Fiber 1 g.

BLUE RIBBON CREAM PIE

The name alone describes this delicious pie.

½ cup/125 ml Watkins Vanilla Dessert Mix
⅔ cup/160 ml white sugar
½ cup/125 ml water
2 egg yolks, slightly beaten
2½ cups/625 ml milk
1 tbsp./15 ml Watkins Vanilla Extract

1¼ cups/325 ml graham cracker crumbs
½ tsp./2.5 ml Watkins Cinnamon
⅓ cup/80 ml melted butter
¼ cup/60 ml white sugar

1 can (21 oz./595 g) blueberry pie filling
1 tsp./5 ml Watkins Almond Extract
1 cup /250 ml sour cream
2 cups/500 ml Vanilla Whipped Cream (page 9)

In medium saucepan, combine dessert mix, sugar, and water. Beat egg yolks into milk and stir into dessert mix mixture; mix until well blended. Cook over medium heat until mixture begins to boil and thicken. Remove from heat and stir in vanilla. Cover surface with plastic wrap; cool until room temperature.

To prepare crust, combine graham cracker crumbs and next 3 ingredients. Spread mixture into a 9-inch/23-cm pie plate. Press onto bottom and up sides of plate ½ inch/1 cm higher than the rim. Bake at 375°F./190°C. for 8 minutes; set on wire rack to cool. Combine blueberry filling and almond extract.

To assemble pie, spread 1 cup/250 ml of the blueberry filling over bottom of crust. Stir sour cream into cooled vanilla filling; spread over blueberries. Spoon remaining blueberry filling evenly over center of pudding; refrigerate at least 2 hours. When ready to serve, pipe or dollop Vanilla Whipped Cream over pie.

Makes 10 servings.

NUTRITIONAL INFORMATION PER SERVING: Calories 470, Protein 5 g, Carbohydrates 58 g, Fat 24 g, Saturated Fat 14 g, Cholesterol 110 mg, Sodium 330 mg, Dietary Fiber 1 g.

CUSTARD PIE

An all time favorite subtly flavored with almonds and nutmeg.

Pastry dough for single crust 9-inch/23-cm pie
4 eggs, slightly beaten
½ cup/125 ml white sugar
¼ tsp./2.5 ml salt
2½ cups/625 ml milk, scalded (heated to just below boiling point)
2 tsp./10 ml Watkins Vanilla Extract
⅛ tsp./0.6 ml Watkins Almond Extract
¼ tsp./1.2 ml Watkins Nutmeg

Place dough in pie plate and chill while making filling. Blend eggs, sugar, and salt. Gradually stir in scalded milk. Add vanilla and almond extracts. Pour into pie shell. Sprinkle with nutmeg. Bake at 400°F./205°C. for 25 to 30 minutes or until knife inserted halfway between outside and center comes out clean. Cool on wire rack 30 minutes, then chill completely in refrigerator.

Makes 10 servings.

NUTRITIONAL INFORMATION PER SERVING: Calories 110, Protein 5 g, Carbohydrates 14 g, Fat 3 g, Saturated Fat 2 g, Cholesterol 93 mg, Sodium 110 mg, Dietary Fiber 0 g.

PEACHES AND CREAM PIE

A layer of cream cheese and peaches top this delicate pie/cake.

¾ cup/180 ml all-purpose flour
1 tsp./5 ml Watkins Baking Powder
½ tsp./2.5 ml salt
¼ cup/60 ml Watkins Vanilla Dessert Mix
⅓ cup/80 ml white sugar
¼ tsp./1.2 ml Watkins Nutmeg
3 tbsp./45 ml butter, softened
1 egg
½ cup/125 ml milk
1 can (16 oz./454 g) sliced peaches, drained
   (reserve juice)

1 package (8 oz./227 g) cream cheese, softened
½ cup/125 ml white sugar
½ tsp./2.5 ml Watkins Vanilla Extract
3 tbsp./45 ml reserved peach juice

1 tbsp./15 ml white sugar
½ tsp./2.5 ml Watkins Cinnamon

Grease bottom of a 9-inch/23-cm deep dish or 10-inch/25-cm pie plate. In large mixing bowl, combine the first 9 ingredients. Beat with an electric mixer at medium speed for 2 minutes. Pour into prepared pan. Place the drained peaches over batter, keeping peaches about ½ to 1 inch/1.2 to 2.5 cm from edge of plate.

In small bowl, combine cream cheese and next 3 ingredients; beat until smooth. Spoon over peaches within same distance from edge. Combine sugar and cinnamon; sprinkle over cream cheese filling. Bake at 350°F./180°C. for 30 to 45 minutes. Cool to room temperature; chill until serving time.

Makes 10 servings.

NUTRITIONAL INFORMATION PER SERVING: Calories 260, Protein 4 g, Carbohydrates 35 g, Fat 12 g, Saturated Fat 8 g, Cholesterol 57 mg, Sodium 310 mg, Dietary Fiber 1 g.

COUNTRY FRUIT TART
WITH CREAM CHEESE CHANTILLY

A home-style fruit tart which will make a grand impression.

PASTRY

1 1/2 cups/375 ml all-purpose flour
1/2 tsp./2.5 ml Watkins Cinnamon
1/4 tsp./1.2 ml salt
1/2 cup/125 ml vegetable shortening
4 to 5 tbsp./60 to 75 ml cold water

Combine flour, cinnamon, and salt in medium mixing bowl. Using a pastry blender or two forks, cut in the shortening until the pieces are the size of small peas. With a fork, stir in enough water to form a smooth dough. Form dough into a ball. Roll out dough, on a lightly floured surface, forming a circle 14 inches/356 cm in diameter. Loosely wrap dough around rolling pin. Unroll onto a 10-inch/25-cm pie plate. Ease pastry into dish. Trim pastry to 1 1/2 inches/38 cm beyond edge of plate.

FILLING

3/4 cup/180 ml white sugar
1/3 cup/80 ml Watkins Vanilla Dessert Mix
3/4 cup/180 ml apricot nectar
3 tbsp./45 ml water
1 tsp./5 ml Watkins Brandy Extract
1/2 tsp./2.5 ml Watkins Cinnamon
1 tbsp./15 ml butter
3 cups/750 ml sliced fresh nectarines
2 cups/500 ml (1 lb./455 g) pitted fresh or
   frozen cherries, thawed
Milk
Powdered sugar

In medium saucepan, combine the sugar and dessert mix; stir in nectar and water. Cook over medium heat until thickened and bubbly. Cook and stir 1 minute more. Remove from heat and stir in all of the remaining ingredients except milk and powdered sugar. Pour filling into pastry-lined dish. Fold the pastry border up and over filling, pleating the pastry to fit (center should be open). Lightly brush pastry with milk. Bake at 375°F./190°C. for 45 to 50 minutes or until pastry is golden. Cool on wire rack. Before serving, sift powdered sugar over pastry edges. Spoon into dessert dishes. Serve with Cream Cheese Chantilly (recipe follows).

Makes 8 servings.

CREAM CHEESE CHANTILLY

1 package (3 oz./85 g) cream cheese, softened
3 tbsp./45 ml white sugar
1 1/2 tsp./7.5 ml Watkins Pure Vanilla Extract
2/3 cup/160 ml heavy whipping cream

Combine cream cheese and sugar in medium bowl; beat until fluffy. Add vanilla and cream and beat until light and fluffy.

Makes 1 cup/250 ml.

NUTRITIONAL INFORMATION PER SERVING: Calories 530, Protein 5 g, Carbohydrates 72 g, Fat 26 g, Saturated Fat 11 g, Cholesterol 42 mg, Sodium 210 mg, Dietary Fiber 2 g.

BAVARIAN APPLE TART

Moist tart apples are nestled in a cream cheese layer atop a sweet crust.

½ cup/125 ml butter, softened
⅓ cup/80 ml white sugar
½ tsp./2.5 ml Watkins White Vanilla Flavor
1 cup/250 ml all-purpose flour
⅛ tsp./0.6 ml Watkins Cinnamon

Cream butter and sugar until light and fluffy. Add vanilla; beat well. Add flour and cinnamon; beat well. Spread onto bottom and 1 inch/2.5 cm up sides of a 9-inch/23-cm springform pan; set aside.

FILLING

1 package (8 oz./227 g) cream cheese
¼ cup/60 ml white sugar
1 egg
1½ tsp./7.5 ml Watkins White Vanilla Flavor
⅓ cup/80 ml white sugar
¾ tsp./3.75 ml Watkins Cinnamon
4 cups/1 liter peeled and sliced Granny Smith apples

Beat together cream cheese and ¼ cup/60 ml sugar until fluffy. Beat in the egg and vanilla; spread onto crust. Combine ⅓ cup/80 ml sugar and cinnamon in a large bowl; toss apples in this mixture. Arrange apples in an attractive pattern on top of the filling. Bake at 450°F./235°C. for 10 minutes. Reduce heat to 400°F./205°C. and bake an additional 25 minutes; cool completely. Keep refrigerated.

Makes 8 servings.

NUTRITIONAL INFORMATION PER SERVING: Calories 390, Protein 5 g, Carbohydrates 44 g, Fat 22 g, Saturated Fat 14 g, Cholesterol 89 mg, Sodium 190 mg, Dietary Fiber 2 g.

CAFÉ VIENNA PIE

A small wedge of this coffee and vanilla flavored pie is sure to satisfy your sweet tooth.

Pastry dough for single 9-inch/23-cm pie crust
1 1/2 cups/375 ml. white sugar
3 tbsp./45 ml all-purpose flour
1 tsp./5 ml Watkins Cinnamon
Dash salt
4 eggs
1/2 cup/125 ml buttermilk
1/2 cup/125 ml butter, softened
2 tsp./10 ml Watkins Vanilla Extract
1 1/2 tsp./7.5 ml Watkins Coffee Flavor
2 squares (1 oz./28 g each) unsweetened chocolate, melted
1/3 cup/80 ml slivered almonds
2 cups Vanilla Whipped Cream (page 9)

Place pastry in pie pan and set aside. Combine sugar, flour, cinnamon, and salt; mix well and set aside. Beat eggs, in a large bowl, until light in color. Beat in dry ingredients. Add buttermilk, butter, vanilla, coffee flavor, and chocolate; mix well. (Filling may look curdled.) Pour into pastry-lined pan. Sprinkle with almonds. Bake at 400°F./205°C. for 30 to 35 minutes or until center is set. Cover edges of crust after 20 minutes to prevent excessive browning. Remove pie from oven and cool completely. Before serving, pipe Vanilla Whipped Cream in a decorative fashion around edges and in center of pie.

Makes 12 servings.

NUTRITIONAL INFORMATION PER SERVING: Calories 400, Protein 5 g, Carbohydrates 41 g, Fat 25 g, Saturated Fat 12 g, Cholesterol 120 mg, Sodium 200 mg, Dietary Fiber 1 g.

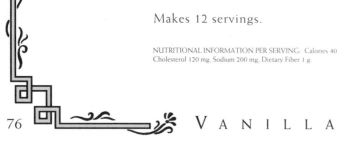

VANILLA

PINEAPPLE UPSIDE DOWN CAKE

Glazed pineapple and cherries top this delicious, moist cake.

3 cans (8.25 oz./234 g each) sliced
  pineapple in own juice (12 slices)
¼ cup/60 ml butter
⅓ cup/80 ml light brown sugar
9 maraschino cherries
1 cup/250 ml all-purpose flour
¾ cup/180 ml white sugar
1½ tsp./7.5 ml Watkins Baking Powder
¼ tsp./1.2 ml salt
¼ tsp./1.2 ml Watkins Nutmeg
¼ cup/60 ml vegetable shortening
½ cup/125 ml milk
2 tsp./10 ml Watkins Vanilla Extract
1 egg
Vanilla Whipped Cream (page 9)

Drain pineapple, reserving 2 tbsp./30 ml of
the juice. In a very heavy or iron ovenproof
10-inch/25-cm skillet, melt butter over
medium heat. Add brown sugar, stirring
until sugar is melted; remove from heat.

Arrange 8 pineapple slices over sugar
mixture, overlapping slightly. Place one
slice in center; fill centers with cherries.
Halve the remaining slices and arrange
around edge of skillet. In large mixing bowl,
combine flour, sugar, baking powder, salt,
and nutmeg. Add shortening and milk; beat
with electric mixer on high 2 minutes. Add
vanilla, egg, and reserved pineapple juice;
beat 2 minutes longer. Pour over pineapple,
spreading carefully. Bake at 350°F./180°C.
for 40 to 45 minutes or until cake tests done.
Let stand on wire rack 5 minutes. Loosen
edges of cake. Cover with serving platter
and invert; remove pan. Serve warm with
Vanilla Whipped Cream.

Makes 8 servings.

NUTRITIONAL INFORMATION PER SERVING: Calories 380, Protein 3 g, Carbohydrates 56 g, Fat 16 g, Saturated Fat 7 g, Cholesterol 54 mg, Sodium 210 mg, Dietary Fiber 0 g.

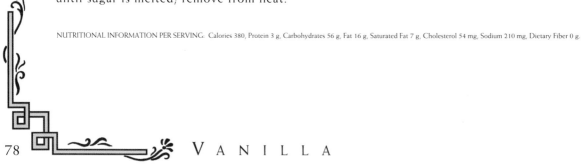

HUMMINGBIRD CAKE

One of Watkins' most requested recipes.

3 cups/750 ml all-purpose flour
2 cups/500 ml white sugar
1 tsp./5 ml baking soda
1 tsp./5 ml salt
1 tsp./5 ml Watkins Cinnamon
3 eggs, beaten
1 cup/250 ml vegetable oil
1 ½ tsp./7.5 ml Watkins Vanilla Extract
1 tsp./5 ml Watkins Butter Flavor
1 can (8 oz./227 g) crushed pineapple,
    undrained
1 cup/250 ml chopped pecans
2 cups/500 ml chopped bananas
Cream Cheese Frosting (recipe follows)
½ cup/125 ml chopped pecans

In large mixing bowl, combine flour and
next 4 ingredients; mix well. Stir in eggs,
oil, vanilla and butter flavor; stir until dry
ingredients are moistened – do not beat.
Fold in crushed pineapple, pecans, and
bananas. Spoon batter into three
9-inch/23-cm round, greased and floured
cake pans. Bake at 350°F./180°C. for 25
to 30 minutes or until a wooden pick
inserted in center comes out clean.
Cool in pans on wire rack 20 minutes,
remove from pans and cool completely.

Spread frosting between layers, on top, and
sides of cake. Sprinkle with chopped pecans.
As flavors blend and intensify upon standing,
refrigerate at least 24 hours before serving.

Makes 12 servings.

CREAM CHEESE FROSTING

1 package (8 oz./227 g) cream cheese, softened
½ cup/125 ml butter, softened
3 ½ cups/875 ml powdered sugar
1 tsp./5 ml Watkins Vanilla Nut Extract

Combine cream cheese and butter, beating
until smooth. Add powdered sugar and
vanilla nut extract; beat until light and fluffy.

NUTRITIONAL INFORMATION PER SERVING: Calories 820, Protein 8 g, Carbohydrates 101 g, Fat 44 g, Saturated Fat 11 g, Cholesterol 95 mg, Sodium 390 mg, Dietary Fiber 3 g.

VANILLA FILLED FUDGE CROWN

Like magic, the vanilla filling appears in center when baked.

1 package (18½ oz./524 g) Swiss or milk chocolate cake mix
1½ tsp./7.5 ml Watkins Cinnamon
1 package (8 oz./227 g) cream cheese, softened
2 tbsp./30 ml butter, softened
1½ tbsp./25 ml Watkins Vanilla Dessert Mix
1 can (14 oz./396 g) sweetened condensed milk
  (not evaporated milk)
1 egg
2 tsp./10 ml Watkins Vanilla Extract

Prepare cake mix as directed on package, adding the cinnamon before mixing. Pour into a well-greased and floured 10 inch/25-cm bundt/tube pan. In small mixing bowl, beat cream cheese, butter, and dessert mix until fluffy. Gradually beat in remaining ingredients until smooth. Pour evenly over cake batter. Bake at 350°F./180°C. for 50 to 55 minutes or until cake tests done. Cool in pan 10 minutes. Remove from pan and place on wire rack; cool thoroughly. Drizzle glaze (recipe below) over cake.

Makes 14 servings.

GLAZE
1 cup/250 ml powdered sugar
1/4 cup/60 ml Watkins Chocolate Dessert Mix
2 tbsp./30 ml vegetable oil
½ tsp./2.5 ml Watkins Vanilla Extract
2 to 4 tbsp./30 to 60 ml warm milk

Combine first 4 ingredients; mix well. Add enough of the milk to achieve desired consistency.

NUTRITIONAL INFORMATION PER SERVING: Calories 390, Protein 6 g, Carbohydrates 56 g, Fat 17 g, Saturated Fat 6 g, Cholesterol 48 mg, Sodium 400 mg, Dietary Fiber 0 g.

WHITE FUDGE CAKE

Vanilla, almond and white chocolate flavors combine to make this very rich cake perfect for special occasions.

¾ cup/180 ml (4 oz./113 g) coarsely
  chopped white chocolate
½ cup/125 ml hot water
2½ cups/625 ml all-purpose flour
1¼ cups/325 ml white sugar
1 tsp./5 ml baking soda
½ tsp./2.5 ml Watkins Baking Powder
¼ tsp./1.2 ml salt
1 cup/250 ml butter, softened
1 cup/250 ml buttermilk or sour milk
3 eggs
1 tsp./5 ml Watkins Vanilla Extract
½ tsp./2.5 ml Watkins Almond Extract
½ cup/125 ml chopped almonds
White Fudge Frosting (recipe follows)

In small saucepan, melt white chocolate and hot water over low heat; cool. In large mixing bowl, combine flour and next 6 ingredients; with electric mixer, mix just until moistened. Then beat 1 minute at medium speed. Add eggs, melted white chocolate mixture, and vanilla and almond extracts. Beat 1 minute at medium speed; stir in almonds. Pour batter into two greased and floured 9-inch/23-cm round cake pans.

Bake at 350°F./180°C. for 30 to 35 minutes or until cake tests done. Cool 15 minutes; loosen edges and carefully remove from pan. Cool completely. Stack layers, bottoms together, spreading white fudge frosting between layers and on top and sides.

WHITE FUDGE FROSTING

¾ cup/180 ml (4 oz./113 g) coarsely
  chopped white chocolate
2 tbsp./30 ml Watkins Vanilla Dessert Mix
1 cup/250 ml milk
1 cup/250 ml butter, softened
1 cup/250 ml white sugar
1 tsp./5 ml Watkins Vanilla Extract

In medium saucepan, combine white chocolate and dessert mix. Blend in milk. Cook over medium heat, stirring constantly until very thick. **Cool completely!** In large mixing bowl, cream butter, sugar, and vanilla; beat until light and fluffy, about 3 minutes Gradually add cooled white chocolate mixture; beat at high speed until the consistency of whipped cream.

NUTRITIONAL INFORMATION PER SERVING: Calories 700, Protein 9 g, Carbohydrates 70 g, Fat 42 g, Saturated Fat 20 g, Cholesterol 140 mg, Sodium 470 mg, Dietary Fiber 1 g.

FRESH APPLE BUNDT CAKE

Apples, vanilla, and nutmeg flavor this moist cake.

Vegetable cooking spray
2 1/2 cups/625 ml all-purpose flour
1 tbsp./15 ml Watkins Baking Powder
1/2 tsp./2.5 ml Watkins Nutmeg
1/4 tsp./1.2 ml baking soda
1 cup/250 ml white sugar
1/2 cup/125 ml butter, softened
1/4 cup/60 ml buttermilk
2 tsp./10 ml Watkins Vanilla Extract
1/2 tsp./2.5 ml Watkins Lemon Extract
1 cup/250 ml egg substitute, thawed if frozen
2 medium Golden Delicious apples, peeled, cored and diced
  (about 2 cups)
Powdered sugar, for dusting

Spray a 10-inch/25-cm bundt/tube pan with cooking spray;
dust with a little flour, then tap out excess. Combine the
flour, baking powder, nutmeg, and soda; set aside. In large
bowl, combine the sugar, butter, buttermilk, vanilla and lemon
extracts; beat until pale and creamy (about 4 minutes).
Alternately add flour mixture and egg substitute; beat until
well blended and fluffy. By hand, stir in apples; spread in
prepared pan. Bake at 350°F./180°C. for 50 to 60 minutes
or until golden brown and cake tests done. Cool in pan on
wire rack 10 minutes. Turn out of pan onto rack and cool
completely. Dust with powdered sugar.

Makes 12 servings.

NUTRITIONAL INFORMATION PER SERVING: Calories 260, Protein 5 g, Carbohydrates 41 g, Fat 8 g, Saturated Fat 5 g,
Cholesterol 21 mg, Sodium 200 mg, Dietary Fiber 1 g.

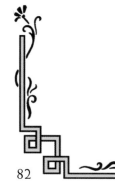

VANILLA

GUILT-FREE POUND CAKE

"Pound cake" got its name from its ingredient list: a pound of sugar, a pound of butter, a pound of eggs, and a pound of flour. Unfortunately, it tends to put extra pounds on anyone who eats it. This alternative recipe is low in fat and cholesterol...but not in flavor.

3 cups/750 ml white sugar
³/₄ cup/180 ml margarine, softened
1¹/₂ cups/375 ml frozen egg substitute,
   thawed or 8 egg whites
1¹/₂ cups/375 ml non-fat plain yogurt or
   low-fat sour cream
1 tsp./5 ml baking soda
4¹/₂ cups/1.15 liters sifted cake flour
¹/₂ tsp./2.5 ml salt
2 tsp./10 ml Watkins Vanilla Extract
1 tsp./5 ml Watkins Butter Flavor
Vegetable cooking spray

Cream sugar and margarine with an electric mixer on medium speed until combined. Gradually add the egg substitute (if using egg whites, add one at a time), beating well. Combine the yogurt and baking soda; mix well and set aside. Combine flour and salt. Add flour mixture and yogurt mixture alternately to egg mixture; beginning and ending with flour mixture. Stir in the vanilla extract and butter flavor. Spoon batter into a 10-inch/25-cm bundt/tube pan coated with cooking spray and lightly floured. Bake at 325°F./165°C. for 1 hour and 20 minutes or until cake tests done.

Cool in pan on wire rack 10 minutes. Remove cake from pan and cool completely.

Makes 20 servings.

Note from kitchen: Use this basic cake recipe as a base to make many different flavored pound cakes using Watkins Flavors and Extracts:

Lemon Pound Cake - Add 2 tsp./10 ml Lemon Extract and decrease the Vanilla Extract to 1 tsp./5 ml.

Coconut Pound Cake - Add 1¹/₂ tsp./7.5 ml Coconut Extract and decrease the Vanilla Extract to 1 tsp./5 ml.

Almond Pound Cake - Add 1¹/₂ tsp./7.5 ml Almond Extract and decrease Vanilla Extract to 1 tsp./5 ml.

Butter Rum - Add 1¹/₂ tsp./7.5 ml Rum Extract and decrease Vanilla Extract to 1 tsp./5 ml.

NUTRITIONAL INFORMATION PER SERVING: Calories 260, Protein 5 g, Carbohydrates 49 g, Fat 5 g, Saturated Fat 1 g, Cholesterol 0 mg, Sodium 220 mg, Dietary Fiber 1 g.

STREUSEL TOPPED APRICOT CAKE

A tender cake lightly flavored with apricots and almonds.

1 package (6 oz./170 g) dried apricots
Boiling water
1 cup/250 ml chopped almonds
½ cup/125 ml brown sugar
3 tbsp./45 ml white sugar
2 tsp./10 ml Watkins Apple Bake Seasoning
½ cup/125 ml all-purpose flour
¼ cup/60 ml butter

1¾ cups/450 ml all-purpose flour
1 cup/250 ml white sugar
¾ tsp./3.75 ml Watkins Baking Powder
½ tsp./2.5 ml baking soda
½ tsp./2.5 ml salt
¾ cup/180 ml butter, softened
⅔ cup/160 ml sour cream
2 eggs
2 tsp./10 ml Watkins Vanilla Extract

In bowl, cover apricots with boiling water; let stand 5 minutes. Drain, then let stand on paper towels; set aside. In bowl, combine almonds and next 3 ingredients; mix well. Set aside ¾ cup/180 ml of this mixture.

For streusel, add the ½ cup/125 ml flour to the remaining almond mixture. Cut in butter with pastry blender or two forks until crumbly; set aside.

In large bowl, combine 1¾ cups/450 ml flour and next 4 ingredients; mix well. Add butter and next 3 ingredients. Using an electric mixer, beat at low speed until moistened. Increase speed to medium and beat 2½ minutes. Spread two thirds of batter into greased 11-x7-inch/28-x18-cm baking dish. Toss reserved ¾ cup/180 ml almond mixture with apricots and sprinkle over batter. Spoon remaining batter over apricot layer; spread evenly. Sprinkle with streusel crumb mixture. Bake at 350°F./180°C. for 55 minutes or until cake tests done. Cool in pan on wire rack.

Makes 12 servings.

NUTRITIONAL INFORMATION PER SERVING: Calories 470, Protein 7 g, Carbohydrates 58 g, Fat 25 g, Saturated Fat 12 g, Cholesterol 83 mg, Sodium 290 mg, Dietary Fiber 3 g.

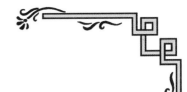

EASY APPLE KUCHEN

Watkins Apple Bake Seasoning lends a unique taste to this all-time favorite.

1/2 cup/125 ml butter, softened
1 3/4 cups/440 ml white sugar, divided
2 eggs
2 1/2 tsp./12.5 ml Watkins Vanilla Extract
1 tsp./5 ml. Watkins Butter Flavor
3 cups/750 ml all-purpose flour
2 tsp./10 ml Watkins Baking Powder
3/4 tsp./3.75 ml salt
1 cup/250 ml milk
5 cups/1.25 liters peeled apple slices
1 tsp./5 ml Watkins Apple Bake Seasoning

Cream butter and 1 1/2 cups/375 ml of the sugar until light and fluffy. Blend in eggs, vanilla and butter flavor. In another bowl, combine the flour, baking powder, and salt; add to creamed mixture alternately with milk, mixing well after each addition. Pour into a greased 13-x9-inch/33-x23-cm baking dish. Arrange apple slices on top. Combine remaining 1/4 cup/60 ml sugar and apple bake seasoning and sprinkle on top. Bake at 375°F./190°C. for 35 to 40 minutes. Serve warm or cold.

Makes 15 servings.

NUTRITIONAL INFORMATION PER SERVING: Calories 280, Protein 4 g, Carbohydrates 49 g, Fat 8 g, Saturated Fat 4 g, Cholesterol 47 mg, Sodium 220 mg, Dietary Fiber 1 g.

TEA CAKE WITH RUM SAUCE

This cake is also delicious served plain or with ice cream.

CRUST

½ cup/125 ml butter, softened
⅓ cup/80 ml white sugar
½ tsp./2.5 ml Watkins Cinnamon
1 cup/250 ml finely chopped pecans
1½ cups/375 ml crushed vanilla wafers

Combine all ingredients, press into bottom and 1 inch/25 cm up sides of 2 well-greased 9-x-5-inch/23-x-13-cm loaf pans; set aside.

BATTER

1 cup/250 ml butter, softened
2 cups/500 ml white sugar
4 eggs
1 cup/250 ml milk
2 tsp./10 ml Watkins Vanilla Extract
2⅔ cups/675 ml all-purpose flour
1½ tsp./7.5 ml Watkins Baking Powder
½ tsp./2.5 ml salt

Beat butter and sugar until light and fluffy. Add eggs; beat well. In separate bowl, combine milk and vanilla. In another bowl, sift together the flour, baking powder, and salt. Add milk mixture and dry mixture alternately to egg mixture; beating well after each addition. Pour batter into crust in pans.

Bake at 350°F./180°C. for 1 to 1¼ hours. Turn out of pans onto a wire rack to cool. Slice cooled cakes; serve with Rum Sauce.

RUM SAUCE

½ cup/125 ml white sugar
1¾ cups/440 ml milk
⅓ cup/80 ml Watkins Vanilla Dessert Mix
¼ cup/60 ml butter
½ tsp./2.5 ml Watkins Rum Extract

In medium saucepan, combine sugar, milk, and dessert mix. Cook over medium heat until mixture comes to a boil. Stir in butter; heat until melted. Remove from heat and stir in rum extract. Serve warm. Sauce can be cooled and then reheated before serving.

Makes 20 servings.

NUTRITIONAL INFORMATION PER SERVING: Calories 500, Protein 6 g, Carbohydrates 62 g, Fat 26 g, Saturated Fat 13 g, Cholesterol 104 mg, Sodium 360 mg, Dietary Fiber 1 g.

  V A N I L L A

CRANBERRY CHEESECAKE

A sweet-tart cranberry topping makes this cheesecake extra special.

CRUST

2 cups/500 ml vanilla wafer crumbs
6 tbsp./90 ml butter, melted

Combine crumbs and butter; press onto bottom and up sides of 9-inch/23-cm springform pan. Bake at 350°F./180°C. for 10 minutes. Reduce oven temperature to 325°F./165°C.

FILLING

3 packages (8 oz./227 g each) cream cheese, softened
¾ cup/180 ml white sugar
1 tbsp./15 ml Watkins White Vanilla Flavor
4 eggs

Combine cream cheese, sugar, and vanilla, mixing at medium speed on electric mixer until well-blended. Add eggs, one at a time, mixing well after each addition; pour over crust. Bake at 325°F./165°C. for 1 hour and 5 minutes. Loosen cake from rim of pan; cool before removing rim of pan. Chill.

CRANBERRY GLAZE

2 cups/500 ml fresh or frozen cranberries
1 cup/250 ml white sugar
½ cup/125 ml water
¼ cup/60 ml white sugar
3 tbsp./45 ml Watkins Vanilla Dessert Mix

Mix cranberries, 1 cup/250 ml sugar, and water; bring to a boil, stirring, for about 2 minutes. Combine ¼ cup/60 ml sugar and dessert mix; stir into cranberry mixture. Cook and stir until boiling. Cool, then chill. Spoon atop cheesecake. Chill 1 to 2 hours. (If desired, cranberries can be spooned on cheesecake after slicing.)

Makes 12 servings.

NUTRITIONAL INFORMATION PER SERVING: Calories 640, Protein 9 g, Carbohydrates 74 g, Fat 36 g, Saturated Fat 19g, Cholesterol 180 mg, Sodium 450 mg, Dietary Fiber 1 g.

MARBLED TERRINE

VANILLA LAYER

1¼ tsp./6 ml unflavored gelatin
2½ cups/625 ml milk, divided
½ cup/125 ml Vanilla Dessert Mix
⅓ cup/80 ml white sugar
⅓ cup/80 ml vanilla milk chips
1 tsp./5 ml Watkins Vanilla Extract

CHOCOLATE LAYER

1¼ tsp./6 ml unflavored gelatin
2½ cups/625 ml milk, divided
½ cup/125 ml Chocolate Dessert Mix
½ cup/125 ml white sugar
⅓ cup/80 ml semi-sweet chocolate chips
1 tsp./5 ml Watkins Vanilla Extract

1 cup/250 ml Vanilla Whipped Cream (page 9)
Chocolate curls, if desired

Line an 8-x4-inch/20-x10-cm loaf pan with plastic wrap; smooth out all wrinkles. Set aside. For vanilla mixture, in medium saucepan combine gelatin and 1 cup/250 ml of the milk; let stand 2 minutes or until softened. Add remaining milk, Vanilla Dessert Mix, and sugar. Cook over medium heat, stirring constantly, until mixture comes to a full boil. Remove from heat; add vanilla milk chips and vanilla; mix well. Place a piece of plastic wrap on top and let stand 15 minutes to cool. Meanwhile, repeat process for chocolate mixture.

To assemble terrine, alternately layer half of vanilla mixture, half chocolate mixture, remaining vanilla mixture and remaining chocolate mixture. Using narrow spatula or knife, gently swirl through mixture to marble. Cover with plastic wrap and refrigerate at least 3 hours before serving. Unmold unto serving plate, removing plastic wrap. Garnish as desired with Vanilla Whipped Cream (try a criss-cross pattern or shell border). If desired, chocolate curls can be placed on top. Cut into slices to serve. Keep refrigerated.

Makes 12 servings.

NUTRITIONAL INFORMATION PER SERVING: Calories 260, Protein 5 g, Carbohydrates 38 g, Fat 11 g, Saturated Fat 8 g, Cholesterol 27 mg, Sodium 240 mg, Dietary Fiber 0 g.

VANILLA ICE CREAM

This recipe is great for those who don't have an ice cream freezer.

½ cup/125 ml egg substitute
1 can (14 oz./397 g) sweetened condensed milk
2 tbsp./30 ml water
4 tsp./20 ml Watkins Vanilla Extract*
2 cups/500 ml heavy whipping cream, whipped

In medium bowl, combine first 4 ingredients; mix
well. Fold egg-milk mixture into whipped cream. Put
into a plastic container, cover and freeze at least 6 hours
or overnight.

Makes approx. 6 cups/1.5 liters, ½ cup/125 ml per serving.

*Try other Watkins Flavors and Extracts. Use level may have
to be adjusted for each.

NUTRITIONAL INFORMATION PER SERVING: Calories 250, Protein 5 g, Carbohydrates 20 g, Fat 18 g, Saturated Fat 11 g,
Cholesterol 66 mg, Sodium 80 mg, Dietary Fiber 0 g.

V A N I L L A

VANILLA GELATO

Gelato is the Italian word for ice cream.
It has a denser texture than its American counterpart.

5 large egg yolks
¾ cup/180 ml white sugar
2 cups/500 ml whole milk
1 cup/250 ml half-and-half
2 tsp./10 ml Watkins Vanilla Extract

Combine egg yolks and sugar in the bowl of an electric mixer.
Beat at medium-high speed until very thick and pale yellow in
color. In medium saucepan, heat milk to a simmer. Add half
the milk to the egg yolk mixture and whisk until blended. Stir
into remaining milk and cook over low heat, stirring constantly,
until mixture coats back of spoon. Remove from heat and
immediately stir in half-and-half. Pass mixture through a fine
strainer into a medium bowl set over an ice bath to chill. Stir
in vanilla. Freeze in an ice cream maker according to
manufacturer's instructions. Store in a plastic container.

Makes 1 qt./liter, ½ cup/125 ml per serving.

NUTRITIONAL INFORMATION PER SERVING: Calories 190, Protein 4 g, Carbohydrates 23 g, Fat 9 g, Saturated Fat 4 g,
Cholesterol 150 mg, Sodium 50 mg, Dietary Fiber 0 g.

LOW-FAT VANILLA ICE MILK

~ ~

You won't believe it's low-fat.

1 cup/250 ml evaporated skim milk
2 cups/500 ml 2% low-fat milk
3/4 cup/180 ml egg substitute, thawed if frozen
3/4 cup/180 ml white sugar
2 to 3 tsp./10 to 15 ml Watkins Vanilla Extract

Combine all ingredients in medium bowl and mix until well-blended and sugar is dissolved. Cover and place in refrigerator; chill 2 hours or longer. Pour mixture into the freezer can of a 2-quart/2-liter hand-turned or electric ice cream freezer. Freeze according to manufacturer's instructions. Spoon frozen mixture into a freezer-safe container, cover and freeze (ripen) at least 1 hour.

Makes 8 servings.

NUTRITIONAL INFORMATION PER SERVING: Calories 150, Protein 7 g, Carbohydrates 26 g, Fat 1 g, Saturated Fat 1 g, Cholesterol 8 mg, Sodium 100 mg, Dietary Fiber 0 g.

QUICK AND EASY MINI FRUIT PIZZAS

Ready to eat in less than 10 minutes.

1 package (3 oz./85 g) cream cheese
1 tbsp./15 ml white sugar
½ tsp./2.5 ml Watkins White Vanilla Flavor
⅛ tsp./0.6 ml Watkins Almond Extract
6 store-bought sugar cookies
Assorted fruit - strawberries, mandarin oranges, bananas,
*   blueberries, kiwis*
Watkins Cinnamon

Place cream cheese in small microwave-safe bowl. Microwave
(HIGH) 30 to 45 seconds or until softened. Stir in sugar and
vanilla and almond extracts. Spread on cookies. Arrange fruit,
as desired, on top of cream cheese layer. Sprinkle with a light
dusting of cinnamon.

Makes 6 servings.

NUTRITIONAL INFORMATION PER SERVING: Calories 120, Protein 2 g, Carbohydrates 10 g, Fat 8 g, Saturated Fat 4 g, Cholesterol 23 mg, Sodium 110 mg, Dietary Fiber 0 g.

VANILLA POACHED PEARS
IN CUSTARD SAUCE

When served in pretty glass bowls, this dish will make a magnificent impression.

6 pears, at room temperature
3 tbsp./45 ml Watkins Vanilla Extract
3 tbsp./45 ml honey

Fill a Dutch oven or 5-quart/5-liter saucepan half full with water. Over high heat, bring to a boil. Meanwhile, core pears from the bottom, leaving stem intact; then peel. Stir the vanilla and honey into the water. Set pears in water. Bring water back to a boil, reduce heat and simmer pears until tender, but not soft (10 to 20 minutes, depending upon ripeness of pears). With slotted spoon, gently remove from poaching liquid and drain well. Cover with plastic wrap and chill until serving time.

CUSTARD SAUCE

1 1/2 cups/375 ml whole milk
4 egg yolks
1/4 cup/60 ml white sugar
Dash of salt
1 tsp./5 ml Watkins Vanilla Extract

Heat milk in top of double boiler over direct heat until tiny bubbles appear around edge of pan. Beat egg yolks, sugar, and salt, mixing well. Pour the hot milk into the egg mixture very slowly, beating constantly. Return mixture to double boiler top; place over hot (not boiling water). Water should not touch pan. Cook, stirring constantly, until mixture is thick enough to coat metal spoon (8 to 10 minutes). Immediately pour custard into a bowl; cover with plastic wrap and set in a larger bowl of ice water to cool. Stir in vanilla. Refrigerate until very cold.

3/4 cup/180 ml Vanilla Whipped Cream (page 9)

To assemble: With pastry tube, fill center of pears with Vanilla Whipped Cream. Divide custard mixture evenly between 6 serving dishes. Place pear upright in center of custard. Pipe remaining whipped topping on sides of pears, as desired. Sprinkle with Watkins Nutmeg. Serve immediately.

Makes 6 servings.

NUTRITIONAL INFORMATION PER SERVING: Calories 310, Protein 5 g, Carbohydrates 49 g, Fat 11 g, Saturated Fat 5 g, Cholesterol 168 mg, Sodium 40 mg, Dietary Fiber 5 g.

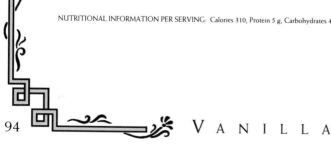

BLACK CHERRY DELIGHT
WITH CUSTARD SAUCE

Just listen for the compliments when you present this beautiful dessert.

2 cans (16.5 oz./468 g) pitted, dark sweet
   cherries in heavy syrup
Water
2 envelopes unflavored gelatin
1½ tbsp./25 ml Watkins Black Cherry
   Punch Concentrate
½ cup/125 ml white sugar
½ cup/125 ml cold water
Custard Sauce (recipe follows)
Chocolate syrup, for garnish
Lemon zest strips, for garnish

In a 2-cup/500-ml glass measure, drain syrup from both cans of cherries; set cherries aside. Add enough water to cherry syrup to measure 2 cups/500 ml of liquid. Place cherry syrup mixture in 2-quart/2-liter saucepan. Evenly sprinkle gelatin over top and let stand 1 minute to soften. Cook over high heat, stirring frequently, until gelatin is dissolved and mixture comes to a boil. Remove from heat and add black cherry concentrate and sugar; stir until sugar is dissolved. Add cold water. Refrigerate until gelatin just begins to thicken sightly; fold in cherries. Spoon into eight ½ cup/125 ml molds. Refrigerate until gelatin is firm, 3 hours or longer.

Meanwhile, prepare Custard Sauce. Cover surface of custard with plastic wrap and refrigerate until well chilled. To serve, unmold each gelatin mold into a large goblet or dessert bowl. Spoon custard around gelatin. Pipe chocolate syrup on top of custard to make an attractive design. Garnish top of gelatin with lemon zest.

Makes 8 servings.

CUSTARD SAUCE

4 egg yolks
½ cup/125 ml white sugar
2 cups/500 ml half-and-half
1 tsp./5 ml Watkins Vanilla Extract

In heavy, 1-quart/1-liter saucepan, beat egg yolks and sugar with wire whisk until well blended. Stir in the half-and-half and cook over medium-low heat, stirring constantly until mixture coats back of spoon, about 25 minutes. (Do not boil, or custard will curdle.) Remove from heat and stir in vanilla.

NUTRITIONAL INFORMATION PER SERVING: Calories 310, Protein 5 g, Carbohydrates 53 g, Fat 9 g, Saturated Fat 5 g, Cholesterol 129 mg, Sodium 34 mg, Dietary Fiber 1 g.

ALMOND MERINGUE TORTE

Garnish this light-textured torte with fresh strawberries and kiwi fruit.

½ cup/125 ml white sugar
½ cup/125 ml vegetable shortening
4 large eggs, separated
5 tbsp./75 ml milk
2 tsp./ 10 Watkins Vanilla Extract
1 cup/250 ml sifted cake flour
1 tsp./5 ml Watkins Baking Powder
¼ tsp./1.2 ml salt

Pinch salt
Pinch cream of tartar
¾ cup/180 ml white sugar
½ cup/125 ml sliced almonds, toasted
2 tsp./10 ml white sugar
½ tsp./2.5 ml Watkins Cinnamon
2 cups/500 ml Vanilla Whipped Cream (page 9)
Assorted fresh fruit, for garnish

In mixing bowl, cream ½ cup/125 ml sugar and shortening until light and fluffy. Add egg yolks, one at a time, beating well after each addition; stir in milk and vanilla. Combine flour, baking powder, and salt; add to creamed mixture and beat until smooth.

Pour into 2 greased 9-inch/23-cm round cake pans. Beat egg whites with a pinch of salt and a pinch of cream of tartar until soft peaks form. Add ¾ cup/180 ml sugar, 1 tbsp./15 ml at a time, until stiff, glossy peaks form.

Divide meringue between pans, spreading over batter and mounding slightly in center. Sprinkle with almonds and the 2 tsp./10 ml sugar mixed with the cinnamon. Bake at 350°F./180°C. for 25 to 30 minutes or until cakes test done. Remove from oven and let stand on wire rack 5 minutes. Turn out onto rack to cool. Using a second rack, turn again so meringue is right-side up. Save any almonds that may fall off for garnish. No more than 6 hours before serving, place 1 layer, meringue side up, on serving plate. Spread with ¾ cup/180 ml Vanilla Whipped Cream. Top with remaining layer, meringue side up, garnish edge with remaining Vanilla Whipped Cream. Garnish with fresh fruit and any reserved almonds.

Makes 12 servings.

NUTRITIONAL INFORMATION PER SERVING: Calories 320, Protein 4 g, Carbohydrates 33 g, Fat 20 g, Saturated Fat 8 g, Cholesterol 99 mg, Sodium 100 mg, Dietary Fiber 1 g.

VANILLA POACHED APPLES
WITH GINGER WHIPPED CREAM

A light refreshing dessert.

2 cups/500 ml white sugar
2 cups/500 ml water
1 tbsp./15 ml Watkins White Vanilla Flavor
¼ tsp./1.2 ml salt
8 medium Golden Delicious apples,
  peeled and cored
Ginger Whipped Cream (recipe follows)
Toasted sliced almonds, for garnish

In large kettle or Dutch oven, bring sugar and water to a boil. Reduce heat and simmer, uncovered, for 5 minutes. Add vanilla and salt; mix well. Place apples in syrup. Cover and simmer 20 minutes or until tender but not soft, turning apples frequently. Remove apples from syrup; cover and chill overnight. Spoon Ginger Whipped Cream into a pastry bag fitted with a star tip; pipe into centers and on tops of apples.

(If desired, apples can be cut into quarters, cutting almost to but not through the bottom before topping with Ginger Whipped Cream. This will give you a "fanning" affect and will make it easier to eat.) Garnish with almonds.

Makes 8 servings.

GINGER WHIPPED CREAM

1 cup/250 ml heavy whipping cream
¼ cup/60 ml white sugar
1 tsp./5 ml Watkins Ginger
1 tsp./5 ml Watkins White Vanilla Flavor

In a medium mixing bowl, beat whipping cream until foamy. Gradually add sugar and Ginger, beating until soft peaks form. Fold in Vanilla.

Makes 2 cups/500 ml.

NUTRITIONAL INFORMATION PER SERVING: Calories 310, Protein 1 g, Carbohydrates 52 g, Fat 12 g, Saturated Fat 7 g, Cholesterol 41 mg, Sodium 80 mg, Dietary Fiber 5 g.

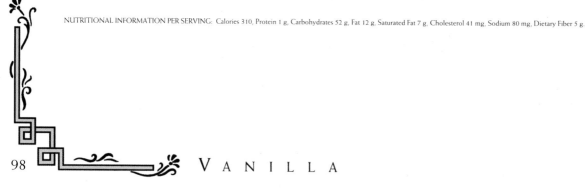

VANILLA

VANILLA CREME WITH STRAWBERRIES

This luscious dessert can also be made with other fresh fruits of the season.

3½ cups/875 ml heavy whipping cream or half-and-half
1½ cups/375 ml white sugar
2 envelopes unflavored gelatin
3 cups/750 ml sour cream
2 to 3 tsp./10 to 15 ml Watkins White Vanilla Flavor
½ tsp./2.5 ml Watkins Banana Flavor
4 cups/1 liter fresh strawberries
2 tbsp./30 ml white sugar
½ tsp./2.5 ml Watkins Strawberry Extract

In large saucepan, combine cream and next 3 ingredients; stir to blend. Cook over low heat, whisking occasionally, until gelatin is dissolved, 12 to 15 minutes. Add vanilla and banana flavor; stir to blend. Pour into greased 8-cup/2-liter mold. Refrigerate until mixture is set, 5 to 6 hours. Wash and remove stems from 3 cups/750 ml of berries. Place in a bowl with sugar and strawberry extract, crush. Chill crushed berries until serving time. Wash and dry remaining berries; chill. Just before serving, unmold Vanilla Creme onto serving platter. Garnish with whole berries. To serve, cut or spoon onto dessert plates and drizzle with crushed berries.

Makes 10 servings.

NUTRITIONAL INFORMATION PER SERVING. Calories 590, Protein 5 g, Carbohydrates 42 g, Fat 46 g, Saturated Fat 28 g, Cholesterol 145 mg, Sodium 70 mg, Dietary Fiber 2 g.

STRAWBERRY DELIGHT

As wonderful to look at as it is to eat.

1 recipe Cream Puff Pastry (page 15)
1 recipe Vanilla Cream Filling (page 10)
3/4 tsp./7.5 ml Watkins Orange Extract
2 cups/500 ml fresh strawberries, sliced

GLAZE
1 tbsp./45 ml Watkins Chocolate Dessert Mix
1 tbsp./45 ml hot water
1/3 to 1/2 cup/80 to 125 ml powdered sugar

Prepare Cream Puff Pastry as directed. Form a ring by placing 8 to 10 spoonfuls of batter, sides touching on greased baking sheet to form an 8-inch/20-cm circle. Bake at 400°F./205°C. for 40 to 50 minutes or until golden brown. Remove from oven; prick puff with sharp knife. Cool completely.

For Filling: Prepare Vanilla Cream Filling as directed, adding orange extract and 1 cup/250 ml of the sliced strawberries.

To Assemble: Place puff on serving plate; slice in half horizontally. Remove any moist dough. Spoon filling into bottom half of puff. Top with remaining strawberries. Replace top of puff. In small bowl, combine dessert mix and hot water; stirring well. Stir in enough powdered sugar to make a smooth glaze. Drizzle over puff. Refrigerate until serving time.

Makes 10 servings.

NUTRITIONAL INFORMATION PER SERVING: Calories 270, Protein 5 g, Carbohydrates 32 g, Fat 14 g, Saturated Fat 8 g, Cholesterol 104 mg, Sodium 280 mg, Dietary Fiber 1 g.

PEANUT BUSTER BAR DESSERT

~⌇~

This makes a very rich dessert, so cut into small pieces.

2 1/2 cups/625 ml crushed round chocolate sandwich cookies
6 tbsp./90 ml butter, softened
2 quarts/2 liters vanilla ice cream or ice milk, slightly softened
2 cups/500 ml powdered sugar
1 1/2 cups/375 ml evaporated milk
2/3 cup/160 ml semi-sweet chocolate chips
1/2 cup/125 butter
1 1/2 tsp./7.5 ml Watkins Vanilla Extract
1 1/2 cups/375 ml Spanish peanuts

In medium bowl, mix cookie crumbs and 6 tbsp./90 ml butter;
pat into 13-x9-inch/33-x23-cm baking dish. Chill in freezer
until set. Pack ice cream into chocolate crust; return to
freezer. Mix the powdered sugar, milk, chocolate chips, and
butter; bring to a boil, stirring constantly, about 8 minutes.
Remove from heat and add vanilla; cool. Sprinkle peanuts
over ice cream, pour sauce over all. Return to freezer
until frozen.

Makes 18 servings.

NUTRITIONAL INFORMATION PER SERVING: Calories 400, Protein 8 g, Carbohydrates 48 g, Fat 28 g, Saturated Fat 12 g,
Cholesterol 57 mg, Sodium 360 mg, Dietary Fiber 1 g.

VANILLA

CHERRY CHEESE SQUARES

Cherries and cheesecake are a favorite flavor combination.

1¼ cups/325 ml all-purpose flour
½ cup/125 ml brown sugar
½ cup/125 ml vegetable shortening
½ tsp./2.5 ml Watkins Butter Flavor
½ cup/125 ml flaked coconut
½ cup/125 ml finely chopped almonds

2 packages (8 oz./ 227 g each) cream
   cheese, softened
⅔ cup/160 ml white sugar
2 eggs, beaten
2 tsp./10 ml Watkins White Vanilla Flavor

1 or 2 cans (21 oz./595 g each)
   cherry pie filling*
½ to 1 tsp./2.5 to 5 ml
   Watkins Almond Extract*
½ cup/125 ml slivered almonds

Combine flour and brown sugar; cut in shortening and butter flavor until fine crumbs form. Stir in coconut and finely chopped almonds. Reserve ½ cup/125 ml mixture for topping. Press remaining mixture into the bottom of a greased 13-x9-inch/33-x23-cm baking dish.

Bake at 350°F./180°C. for 12 to 15 minutes or until lightly browned. Meanwhile, for filling, beat the cream cheese, white sugar, eggs and vanilla in mixing bowl until smooth. Spread over the hot crust. Bake an additional 15 minutes. Combine pie filling and almond extract and spread on top of cream cheese filling. Combine reserved crumbs and slivered almonds; sprinkle over cherries. Bake 15 minutes more. Cool on wire rack. Refrigerate until serving time.

Makes 24 servings.

*Note from kitchen: The amount of cherries can be added to your own personal taste. For more cheesecake flavor, use one can of cherries and ½ tsp./2.5 ml almond extract; for a more intense cherry flavor, use 2 cans of cherries and 1 tsp./5 ml almond extract.

NUTRITIONAL INFORMATION PER SERVING: Calories 260, Protein 4 g, Carbohydrates 30 g, Fat 15 g, Saturated Fat 6 g, Cholesterol 38 mg, Sodium 80 mg, Dietary Fiber 2 g.

WHITE CHOCOLATE TRUFFLES

Store these delectable truffles in the refrigerator.

2 cups/500 ml vanilla milk chips
¼ cup/60 ml sour cream
1½ tsp./7.5 ml Watkins Pure Vanilla Extract
¼ to ½ tsp./1.2 to 2.5 ml Watkins Almond Extract
Powdered sugar, cocoa, or melted semi-sweet chocolate

Melt vanilla milk chips in small saucepan over low heat, stirring constantly; remove from heat. Stir in sour cream, vanilla and almond extracts; mix well. (If mixture begins to stiffen, return to low heat until mixture is smooth.) Refrigerate approximately 60 minutes or until mixture is firm enough to handle, stirring occasionally. Form mixture into ¾-inch/2-cm balls. Roll some in powdered sugar, some in cocoa, or leave plain and pipe on melted chocolate in an attractive pattern on top with a decorating bag. Store in an airtight container in refrigerator.

Makes 60 truffles, one per serving.

NUTRITIONAL INFORMATION PER SERVING: Calories 50, Protein 1 g, Carbohydrates 5 g, Fat 2 g, Saturated Fat 2 g, Cholesterol 0 mg, Sodium 20 mg, Dietary Fiber 0 g.

MICROWAVE CARAMELS

Quick and easy to make.

Butter for greasing baking dish
1 cup/250 ml (2 sticks) butter, melted
1 pound/454 g (2¼ cups/575 ml packed) brown sugar
1 can (14 oz./397 g) sweetened condensed milk
1 cup/250 ml light corn syrup
1 tbsp./15 ml Watkins Vanilla Extract

Butter a 13-x9-inch/33-x23-cm baking dish; set aside.
Combine first 4 ingredients in 3-quart/3-liter microwave-safe
bowl. Microwave (HIGH) 17 minutes, stirring every 5 minutes.
Remove from microwave; stir in vanilla. Pour into prepared
baking dish; cool. When set, cut into squares and wrap
individually in waxed paper. Store in refrigerator.

Makes 116 1-inch/25-cm pieces, one per serving.

NUTRITIONAL INFORMATION PER SERVING: Calories 50, Protein 0 g, Carbohydrates 8 g, Fat 2 g, Saturated Fat 1 g,
Cholesterol 5 mg, Sodium 20 mg, Dietary Fiber 0 g.

OLD FASHIONED TAFFY

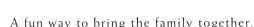

A fun way to bring the family together.

3 cups/750 ml white sugar
1 1/4 cups/325 ml boiling water
1/4 cup/60 ml butter
2 tbsp./30 ml white vinegar
1 tsp./5 ml Watkins Vanilla Extract
1/4 to 1 tsp./1.2 to 5 ml of your favorite
    Watkins Extract or Flavor
Few drops food coloring, if desired

Combine sugar, water, butter, and vinegar; heat to boiling, stirring occasionally. Cook over medium heat without stirring, to 260°F./130°C. on candy thermometer (hard-ball stage). Remove from heat; stir in vanilla, any other extract or flavor of choice, and food coloring. Pour into 13-x-9-inch/33-x-23-cm buttered pan or large buttered platter. Turn the mixture toward the center with a spatula as edges firm. When cool enough to handle, pull taffy with lightly buttered hands until satiny, light in color, and stiff. Stretch into long strips 1/2 inch/1.25 cm wide. Cut into 1-inch/2.5-cm pieces with scissors. Wrap pieces individually in waxed paper. (Candy must be wrapped to hold its shape.)

Makes about 100 pieces, one per serving.

NUTRITIONAL INFORMATION PER SERVING: Calories 30, Protein 0 g, Carbohydrates 6 g, Fat 0 g, Saturated Fat 0 g, Cholesterol 1 mg, Sodium 4 mg, Dietary Fiber 0 g.

MIXED NUT TOFFEE ROLL

An incredibly rich-tasting treat.

1 1/4 cups/325 ml white sugar
3/4 cup/180 ml dark corn syrup
3/4 cup/180 ml chunky-style peanut butter
1 tsp./5 ml Watkins Vanilla Extract
1 tsp./5 ml Watkins Vanilla Nut Extract
1 can (8 oz./227 g) unsalted or salted dry-roasted mixed nuts
1 cup/150 ml chopped unsalted or salted dry-roasted peanuts

Grease a 13-x9-inch/33-x-23-cm baking dish; set aside. In heavy 2-quart/2-liter saucepan, over medium heat, cook sugar and corn syrup, stirring constantly, until sugar is melted and mixture comes to a boil. Boil one minute, stirring constantly. Remove from heat, stir in peanut butter, and extracts. Stir until completely blended; stir in mixed nuts only. Pour into prepared pan; let stand until cool enough to handle. Divide mixture in half, shape each half into a log 12 inches/30 cm long and about 1 1/2 inches/4 cm in diameter. Roll logs in chopped peanuts to coat completely. Wrap logs tightly in plastic wrap to hold shape, refrigerate about 1 1/2 hours or until firm. Using a sharp knife, cut into 3/8 inch / 1 cm-thick slices. Store between waxed paper in a tightly covered container in a cool, dry location.

Makes 60 pieces, one per serving.

NUTRITIONAL INFORMATION PER SERVING: Calories 80, Protein 2 g, Carbohydrates 9 g, Fat 5 g, Saturated Fat 1 g, Cholesterol 0 mg, Sodium 20 mg, Dietary Fiber 1 g.

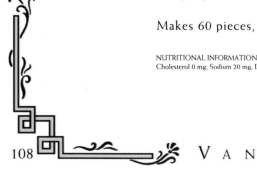

V A N I L L A

CHOCOLATE FUDGE

Smooth and creamy, just like Grandma used to make.

2½ cups/625 ml white sugar
½ cup/125 ml butter
1 can (5 oz./142 g) evaporated milk
  (2/3 cup/160 ml)
1 jar (7 oz./198 g) marshmallow creme
  (2 cups/500 ml)
1 package (12 oz./340 g) semi-sweet
  chocolate chips
½ cup/125 ml chopped walnuts
1 tsp./5 ml Watkins Vanilla Extract
1 tsp./5 ml Watkins Vanilla Nut Extract

Line a 9-inch/23-cm square baking dish with foil so foil extends over sides of pan; spray with vegetable cooking spray. In large saucepan, combine sugar, butter, and milk. Bring to a boil over medium heat, stirring constantly. Continue boiling 5 minutes, stirring constantly; remove from heat. Add marshmallow creme and chocolate chips; blend until smooth. Stir in walnuts and extracts. Pour into prepared pan. Cool to room temperature. Score fudge into 48 squares. Refrigerate until firm.

Remove fudge from pan by lifting foil; carefully peel off foil. Cut with knife through scored lines. Store in airtight container in the refrigerator with waxed paper between layers.

Makes 48 pieces, one per serving.

Note from kitchen:
Also try the following recipe...

BUTTERSCOTCH FUDGE

Substitute 12 oz./340 g butterscotch chips for chocolate chips, pecans for walnuts, and Watkins Butterscotch Flavor for Vanilla Nut Extract.

...and create your own favorites with other Watkins Extracts and Flavors.

NUTRITIONAL INFORMATION PER SERVING: Calories 120, Protein 1 g, Carbohydrates 18 g, Fat 5 g, Saturated Fat 3 g, Cholesterol 6 mg, Sodium 20 mg, Dietary Fiber 0 g

MICROWAVE PEANUT BRITTLE

～ン～

You don't need a candy thermometer to make this crispy brittle.

1 ½ cups/375 ml unsalted dry-roasted peanuts
1 cup/250 ml white sugar
½ cup/125 ml light corn syrup
⅛ tsp./0.6 ml salt
1 tbsp./15 ml butter
1 tbsp./15 ml Watkins Vanilla Extract
1 tbsp./15 ml Watkins Vanilla Nut Extract
1 tsp./5 ml baking soda

Lightly grease a large baking sheet; set aside. In large glass mixing bowl, combine peanuts, sugar, corn syrup, and salt. Microwave (HIGH) 7 to 9 minutes until mixture is bubbling and peanuts are brown. Quickly stir in butter and extracts. Microwave (HIGH) 2 to 3 minutes longer. Add baking soda; stir quickly just until mixture is foamy. Pour immediately onto prepared baking sheet spreading to desired thinness. Let cool about 15 minutes or until firm. Break peanut brittle into pieces; store in airtight containers.

Makes 1¼ pounds/570 g, 1 oz./28 g per serving.

NUTRITIONAL INFORMATION PER SERVING: Calories 130, Protein 3 g, Carbohydrates 19 g, Fat 5 g, Saturated Fat 1 g, Cholesterol 0 mg, Sodium 60 mg, Dietary Fiber 1 g.

DIVINITY

A holiday favorite.

2½ cups/625 ml white sugar
½ cup/125 ml light corn syrup
¼ tsp./2.5 ml salt
½ cup/125 ml water
2 egg whites
2 tsp./10 ml Watkins White Vanilla Flavor
Chopped nuts, optional

Mix together sugar, corn syrup, salt, and water in heavy
2-quart/2-liter saucepan. Place over medium heat and stir
until sugar dissolves. Cover until mixture begins to boil.
Remove cover and boil, without stirring, until mixture reaches
260°F./130°C. (hard-ball stage). Just before syrup reaches this
level, beat egg whites with an electric mixer until stiff. Pour
syrup slowly over beaten egg whites, beating constantly on
high speed of electric mixer. Add vanilla and continue beating
until mixture begins to thicken and hold its shape, 4 to 5
minutes. Add nuts, if desired, and quickly drop by teaspoonfuls
onto buttered waxed paper. Let stand until cool. Store in
airtight containers.

Makes about 40 pieces, one per serving.

Note from kitchen: For different flavors of divinity, try
substituting 2 tsp./10 ml Watkins Strawberry Extract for the
White Vanilla, or substitute 1 tsp./5 ml Watkins Cherry Extract
and chopped well-drained maraschino cherries for the White
Vanilla and nuts, or add 1 tsp./5 ml Watkins Orange Extract
and grated orange peel.

NUTRITIONAL INFORMATION PER SERVING: Calories 60, Protein 0 g, Carbohydrates 15 g, Fat 0 g, Saturated Fat 0 g, Cholesterol 0 mg, Sodium 20 mg, Dietary Fiber 0 g.

INDEX